SEEDS TO SUCCESS

SEEDS TO SUCCESS

How to Produce Results in Life and at Work

JOE PETTIT

ARROW PRESS

Hardcover: 978-1-951475-22-2
Paperback: 978-1-951475-21-5
Ebook: 978-1-951475-23-9

Library of Congress Control Number: 2022916150

Arrow Press Publishing
Summerville, SC
www.arrowpresspublishing.com

DEDICATION

I want to express appreciation for my wife, Damaris. You make me so much better. This book is as much yours as it is mine. Thank you for encouraging me to write Seeds to Success. I love you.

A big thank you to my children, Lexxie, OV, Isabella, and Joseph, for inspiring me to do more, be more, and give more. Your support and encouragement make me better. We are better together. Dad loves you!

Thank you Mom, for showing me what unconditional love looks like and for never allowing me to settle for anything less than success. My admiration for you far exceeds my words, but know this, I love you, Mom.

Thank you Dad, for showing me why we should never give up hope and why relationships are life's greatest joy.

ACKNOWLEDGMENTS

Thank you to every person who purchased this book to read or to give as a gift. I wrote this book specifically for you. The things you're capable of doing are unmatched. As you succeed, always remember to give back and keep planting seeds to success. Share stories and use #SeedsToSuccess to inspire others to win at home and at work.

Thank you to all family, friends, enemies, and past colleagues for influencing this accomplishment in some way or another.

Thank you, Arrow Press Publishing, for turning this project into a gem. The entire team helped make a dream come true and it's better than I ever imagined.

Thank you to all my personal manuscript reviewers. I appreciate your time, energy, and effort offering suggestions, being a sounding board, and for pressing me to write this book. Let's go!

Thank you, Farmer Katie Donohoe, for taking the time to teach me about farming and doing it with an optimistic outlook.

Thank you Jesus, for saving me and giving me an opportunity to turn over a new leaf. You gave me a new life and a mission to help others.

Thank you to all farmers for fueling our nation and an extra bit of gratitude for all the smaller farms doing their thing while positively impacting their communities.

CONTENTS

INTRODUCTION

S eeds are non-threatening, inexpensive, and they are everywhere you look. They come in varied sizes, shapes, and colors, yet they all have one thing in common. They are not
identified by what they are, but by what they'll become.

Perhaps this is why the word "seed" is prefaced by its mature form. It's an apple seed, a pumpkin seed, a sunflower seed.
Yes, it's an identifier, but it's more than that. It's an indicator of
what will be. If the seed falls on good soil and is properly treated,
it will grow into something beautiful and bountiful. If the seed is
ignored, it will never achieve its destiny. It will never mature into
an apple tree, a pumpkin, or a sunflower. The original goal for
the seed was always maturity and multiplication.

Everyone who leads an organization looks for people who
are mature enough to contribute quickly, advance the bottom line,
and alleviate the burden of work. The more mature the organization, the less they consider seed-form employees. It's expected
that a start-up maximizes undeveloped talent, but should a Fortune 100 company take the same approach? I would argue that it
should.

Failing to recognize the apple orchard that exists in the apple seed is a major hindrance in fostering generational growth, both relationally and professionally. Developing a person, a company, a culture, an environment, or a non-profit organization requires a leader who is able to "see it before they see it". They need to be able to recognize potential in themselves and others, viewing every employee, co-worker, oversight, or direct report as someone with eternal value, purpose, and ability.

When you pick an apple off a tree, you seldom think about the thousands of seeds that fail to fulfill their destiny. No, you stand in the shade of the apple tree and enjoy the fruit. If we're honest, many of us would rather just enjoy the fruit than take part in the labor.

Success is no different. There are success seeds. In seed form, you'd not see the overwhelming accomplishments forming within. If we're not careful we'll desire the orchard but never plant, water, or cultivate the seed to produce a single tree. Success seeds are orchards in seed form. They are small, seemingly insignificant choices that lead to fulfillment.

It's fascinating to think that most fruits contain seeds. That means within their mature form is the ability to reproduce its own kind. This is why leadership development

YOU WILL OFTEN KNOW WHAT KIND OF LEADER YOU ARE BY THE FRUIT YOU PRODUCE.

is so crucial within an organization. You'll often know what kind of leader you are by the fruit you produce. When you develop, those around you also develop.

John Maxwell calls this the Law of the Lid. He states, "I believe that success is within the reach of just about everyone. But I also believe that personal success without leadership ability brings only limited effectiveness. Without leadership ability, a person's impact is only a fraction of what it could be with good leadership. Your accomplishments will be restricted by your ability to lead others. By raising your leadership ability — without necessarily increasing your success dedication at all — you can increase your original effectiveness a tremendous amount. That's because leadership has a multiplying effect."[1]

To be effective your leadership must develop, much like the seed. When developed properly it will multiply. One apple becomes an apple tree, which becomes an apple orchard. Raise your leadership and you'll multiply your results.

IF YOU LOOK IN THE MIRROR AND ONLY SEE A SEED, YOU'RE IN LUCK. THE HARVEST IS NOT FAR BEHIND.

Seeds to Success will provide you with simple, easily incorporated steps to help you identify your potential. It details how to take action and provides practical direction to nurture your personal and professional growth to receive the best results possible. It provides clear and concise transformational methods for you, your family, and your organization to produce better results in life and at work.

If you look in the mirror and only see a seed, you're in luck. Your journey is just beginning and the harvest is not far behind.

CHAPTER 1

Success is Yours to Produce

W hat she said did not coincide with the way she looked. Perhaps that's what made her determination so palpable.

"It's. Not. Over," my mom prophetically declared. Little did I know, those words would forever shape my life.

I'm the product of two hardworking parents. My mother was a seamstress and my father was a welder. For 48 years he built things with his hands, but in December 1990 my father tore our family apart.

Our house was a two-bedroom, one bathroom house. My father was remodeling the home at the time and everything was bare; all the sheetrock had been torn off the walls. I can still see those piles of sawdust swept into the corner. Our house was being demolished, but so was our family.

The only time I can recall our entire family sitting at our kitchen table was this instance. My mother was sobbing in anticipation of what was about to happen. My father told us that because of the choices he made, because of the seeds he planted, we would be forced to live in a home without him. My parents were getting a divorce.

As an 8-year-old boy, my world fell apart. I was faced with the realization that I would never see my father again in our home. I would have to learn how to live without him. The next morning, staring at our popcorn ceiling, I tried to convince myself this was a nightmare, but I knew better. I walked into the kitchen the same as I had the night before. I sat in the same seat as I had the night before.

My southern mom always cooked a hot breakfast for us. Growing up I ate bacon, eggs, and grits, but this morning was different. Cereal was never on mom's menu, but this morning there was a box on the table. It was just another sign that things were changing. I tried to pour the cereal, but it went everywhere. I missed the bowl completely and the cereal fell on the table and floor. In an act of frustration, anger, and overwhelming emotion I stood up and began to crush every piece of cereal on the floor.

WE ARE GOING TO GET THROUGH THIS. IT'S. NOT. OVER.

I looked at my mom and said, "This is how I feel! My heart is crushed! It's over." She looked at me and said, "Joseph Ray! We are going to get through this! Son, IT'S. NOT. OVER."

Successful leaders begin with the end in mind, and my mother definitely had the end in mind when she declared, "it's not over." She refused to forfeit our future because of someone else's poor decision. She took responsibility and committed to producing a successful life. We didn't realize at the time how long it would take for this success to come to fruition, how long it would take for the seed to mature into something beautiful.

The seeds to success are within your reach but you must also begin with the end in mind. You must decide who you want to be and become the author of your own success story.

The Farmer in the Dell

We are no longer an agrarian society, so to truly understand the leadership lessons found in the seed we must first break down the farmer's approach to success. The farmer knows what they want to produce before the seed is purchased or planted. They have a vision for each square foot of barren land. A farmer sees the harvest before others can see a seedling emerging from the ground. They can "see it before they see it".

The average person sees unused, uninhabited land devoid of anything worthwhile, but a farmer knows the potential within the land. They will have to add nutrients to the soil, pull the weeds, and deliberately plant the seeds to produce a harvest that will benefit their family and community. The farmer must tend to the seed daily, nurturing them to ensure optimal growth. Water and

VISIONARY LEADERS UNDERSAND EACH DECISION TO INVEST IN A TEAM MEMBER WILL REAP A BENEFIT.

sunlight are necessary for the process to begin. The seed's embryo is awakened and roots shoot into the dark, damp soil. A farmer's actions become evident to others as the seedling pokes through the dirt, unfurling green leaves for the world to see. Even with the promise of early success, people don't see what the farmer sees.

When it's time to gather the harvest every doubter, bystander, and critic gathers around hoping to receive the fruit of the farmer's labor. Naysayers become supporters and cynics become colleagues.

Leadership is identical to the farmer's approach in that it requires planning, preparing, planting, and producing, which will be covered in greater detail when we unveil the Seeds to Success Framework. A visionary leader sees the potential from small choices sown into team members. Each decision to invest in a team member will reap a benefit. On the other hand, neglecting to sow into a team member will produce results as well. These results, referred to as "weeds," are detrimental to an organization's success.

Just as a farmer wants to produce a high-quality yield, leaders want to see healthy organizational growth. The self-aware leaders understand that ultimate success is not found in the bottom line. It is found in developing their team and challenging them to achieve the best version of themselves. Both elements are essential for a profitable and sustainable business.

Simon Sinek summarizes this sentiment perfectly in his book, The Infinite Game. He states, "Leaders are not responsible for the results, leaders are responsible for the people who are responsible for the results. And the best way to drive performance in an organization is to create an environment in which information can flow freely, mistakes can be highlighted and help can be offered and received."[1]

Great leaders are responsible for sowing seeds and fostering an optimal environment for growth. The leader needs to create a clear plan and vision for what they want to achieve. They must prepare the soil — the workplace culture — and add or remove what's needed for long-term growth. Only then should a leader plant a seed of action into their business.

Every organization wants positive results but they rarely want to do the work required to produce those results. The process is simple, but simple does not mean easy.

We've been coaxed to believe the fallacy that success is straightforward and uncomplicated, requiring minimal effort. You experience it daily as you are bombarded with advertisements about the next new thing. We are obsessed with shortcuts. We want the quickest possible path to success and are willing to pay exorbitant amounts of money to get there. For instance, according to the Boston Medical Center, Americans spend 33 billion dollars a year on weight loss products, yet nearly two-thirds of Americans are overweight or obese.[2]

People want the seed to produce overnight and when it doesn't, or when it requires more work than they had anticipated, they abandon the process. If only they realized that the process is the reward. Those who are most satisfied at work and home are those who have committed to the process. They understand that unreasonable results will require unreasonable effort and they are ok with it. They won't plant a seed today and expect an orchard tomorrow, but rest assured they will check on that seed daily, prepared to course correct as needed to see the seed grow.

We don't just see this trend in the weight loss industry. We see it in our ambition for fast wealth. Bill Keen of Forbes examined our attraction to get-rich-quick schemes and in doing so discovered several common habits of successful investors.

First, they work their plan. They don't panic when the market goes down or get overly excited when it goes up. They're steady. Do they make adjustments to the plan as they go? Absolutely — but they always stick to the plan.

They don't chase after the latest "get rich quick" opportunity. They know where they are, where they want to get to and the path that's most likely to lead them there. All the detours along the way are just distractions that could lead them away from their goal of financial independence.[3]

Can success be achieved? Of course, but you must first define what success means to you. Your employer, spouse, parent, or friend may contend for their own definitions of success and insist you follow, but you don't want to get to the end of your life having reached the top of the corporate ladder only to realize you were climbing the wrong ladder.

Success is defined as "the accomplishment of an aim or purpose." What are you aiming at?

- As a young student, I aimed for the honor roll.
- As a teenager, I aimed to earn a college football scholarship.
- As an adult, I aimed to be married, have a family, and buy a house.
- As a leader, I aimed for top pay, to work for a successful company, and to make a positive impact on those I led.

Not having a target in mind, or a purpose to guide you, is detrimental to your success and will derail your personal growth.

Repoed

When I saw my wife, Damaris, in the summer of 2005, things changed. I was immediately captured by her beauty and her presence. She stole my heart from day one. We met during my young management career at Red Lobster in Pineville, NC.

In 2007, after being together couple of years, Damaris and I married. We had little to nothing. When the Beatles wrote the song, "All You Need is Love," they clearly didn't have our relationship in mind. We were drowning in bad debt and excelled in poor decision making, but while our pathetic choices nearly wrecked our marriage, it was through these trials that we matured.

SUCCESS IS DEFINED AS THE ACCOMPLISHMENT OF AN AIM OR **PURPOSE**. **WHAT ARE YOU AIMING AT?**

I never would have thought our relationship would endure so many ups and downs. There are stages I'd love to erase, but the challenging times are what motivated me later in life. We lived in a single-wide trailer yet struggled to pay the $220 per month rent. We both worked but our financial mismanagement nearly cost our family everything.

In 2011, we experienced a wake-up call that shook me to my core. On a cold, quiet, Sunday evening in January we were awakened by the sound of dogs barking several houses away. Their yelps echoed through the flimsy, tall pine trees. Our two oldest children were asleep. Damaris and I were preparing for the upcoming week.

Suddenly, the sound of a truck in our driveway broke the winter night's silence. I peeked outside into the dark, but couldn't make out who was there.

"How can I help you?" I yelled out the front door.

The driver responded, "The bank sent us here to pick up your cars. You didn't make your payments, and now your cars are being repossessed."

How could this be?

My pleas for mercy fell on deaf ears as they rolled the cars onto their flatbed tow truck. I lost both cars that night and woke up the following morning to two children who needed a ride to school, a wife who had no ride to work and no answers or vehicles to make it happen.

I felt defeated, depressed, and drained. In a moment I was back at that kitchen table, 8 years old, afraid, and hopeless.

Although things got worse before they got better, this moment was my first turning point. I learned that in order to succeed I needed to:

- Take responsibility for my life.
- Live life with a plan.
- Do what's right over what feels right in the moment.

Less than 10 years later we were in a position to buy our first home. Like most homebuyers, we had some "must haves." It was our dream to own a home and our requirements were modest. We wanted a place for our children to play, space to host parties and a yard with full sunlight so I could have a raised bed vegetable garden.

The fifth house we saw had it all. It has one of the largest lots in the neighborhood with full sun, a community pool and a playground adjacent to the backyard, and an open floor plan with lots of natural light beaming in. It was our ideal first home purchase.

We finally completed the arduous closing process and officially became homeowners. And, yes, the hosting space inside and the yard made this Lowcountry South Carolina address perfect.

I stood in the July sun visualizing which vegetables and herbs I'd grow long before I even thought about unpacking the brown cardboard boxes or the storage box truck. Would I grow pickling cucumbers or English cucumbers? How many hot peppers would I need to plant? Tomatoes? Oh yes, I can grow 10 different varieties of tomatoes here.

I saw everything I wanted to produce as I stood on the manicured centipede grass. As my teenagers came outside to see why I was staring at the empty yard, I excitedly rattled off every plant I wanted to grow and where it would be planted. "But, we have to act fast because it's July and the growing season is half over" I told them.

Their teenage excitement (or should I say, lack thereof) indicated my vision was hard for others to see, or perhaps their passion wasn't on the same level as mine? Either way, I continued moving towards each new spot marking the garden measurements with one foot, toe-to-heel, after another.

An adult trying to interest a young mind into growing vegetables has always been a hard sell. I clearly remember being a teenager and having little enthusiasm for growing vegetables, a sharp contrast to today.

As an adolescent growing up in Putman, a small community on the outskirts of Buffalo, South Carolina, I helped my grandmother, Matrel (O'Shields) Stribling during the summer months pick yellow squash, snap green beans and cut slimy okra my grandfather, Robert Franklin Stribling, grew. We'd even leave "the hill" and travel three doors down to admire my grandmother's younger brother, Uncle Ryan's 10-foot-high corn stalks lining Highway 215.

After leaving his house, we'd walk to his neighbor's house where my grandmother's youngest brother, Uncle Emmette, lived. He enjoyed growing a variety of vegetables as well, but I always remember him offering hot peppers nearly every visit. Looking back, he knew I'd decline the peppers because of the unforgiving heat that rivaled any pepper on the Scoville scale. He enjoyed the playful teasing and seeing my reaction.

My grandparents and uncles' gardens produced every year, as if it was a personal guarantee made by God. To a young mind, the harvest seemed to happen with little work.

What was it? How could they produce a bountiful harvest year after year? I wondered. It wasn't until my restaurant days when the farm to table movement exploded in the South circa 2008 that I received my answer. Some will argue this date, but this is when the movement found me. I thought about my grandparents' garden again and began to understand their success.

As the focus turned towards a deep interest in where we get our food and who grew our food, I realized the process my ancestors went through wasn't magic but a labor of love, sweat and necessity.

My interest piqued. I took a job with a restaurant focused on bringing the farm into their restaurant. There was a raised bed, herb garden lining the front entrance as customers walked in for lunch. One of my opening duties was to water the plants and tend to each plant's wellbeing.

Watering needed to happen one to two times a day to quench the young basil's thirst as it survived the beaming South Carolina sun. This was an easy task but an important one. If not done consistently the plant stood no chance of survival. It was a perfect task for someone who never planned or planted a full garden before.

The vision a farmer has for their garden, and the detail to which they tend it, came alive inside me. My attention was fixed on Jeffrey, the house grower. He carefully pulled the clover ground cover and explained he was turning the garden to allow the clover to release its nutrients in the soil.

He brought in topsoil and emptied 5-gallon white plastic buckets with disintegrated restaurant kitchen scraps to the un-planted beds. He pointed at the empty mess of a garden bed and explained that pole beans would climb the columns, basil plants would line the perimeter, and patty pan squash would fill the middle.

Jeffrey quickly pointed out that we had to prepare the soil a few days before a seed could be sowed directly into the ground. Once the preparation was complete, seeds were sown, and love was given to the plants on a daily basis.

I remembered from my childhood the bright yellow squash flowers opening, as if to say, "Good morning" and "Thank you" for all the love shown.

As my love for gardening grew I realized while I appreciated the end result, it's the process leading up to the harvest where growth happens. To produce a harvest it requires seed, soil, a farmer, and the proper season. Without the winter's frost, soil couldn't transform and hold a cover crop.

Cover crops, used by farmers for decades, have seen a resurgence and increase of acres planted since 2012. According to the U.S. Department of Agriculture Census of Agriculture, which is taken every five years, eight states more than doubled their cover crop usage from 2012 to 2017. The greatest rise was in Iowa, a 156% increase.

Cover crops, such as clover and types of rye and radishes, are planted when fields would otherwise lay fallow to protect soil from erosion and help build up and put nutrients back into the soil.[4]

Without spring, a tender seed wouldn't have time to grow. Summer brings all the things most plants need, and fall brings cooler weather to allow the farmer to harvest.

As I watched this beautiful circle of creation unfold, I discovered something was happening to me as well. I discounted the lessons learned for years until I began to see what nature taught about leadership and how to produce consistent, healthy results.

The lessons were right in front of me. As I approached the rewards, I began to see how the principles of seed sowing and harvest applied to multiple walks of life.

As you journey through this book, open your mind to what's possible inside of your organization, your personal life and your professional growth. Like a garden, there are no shortcuts for hard work, consistency, and having faith in a seed's potential.

LET 'EM KNOW THE HARVEST IS COMING!

Take your time. Don't go too fast. Open your mind to what's possible and give yourself grace as you plow towards a bountiful harvest.

When I was young my father was a giant. He is 6' 8", his hands were as hard as a metal railing and his heart was as cold as an ice cube. At least that's what I thought. But several years ago, something unexpected happened. My father began to change and turn over a new leaf. He realized life is short and he'd better make the most of it. For the last few years, he's been more involved with me and my family than the first thirty-six years of my life.

He has never apologized for what happened when I was eight years old, but he doesn't have to. The change is undeniable. He made a decision to produce a new life with us and I'm forever grateful for it.

Your life and your success is within your control. Your business may not have grown the way you'd hoped it would. You may not have gotten that promotion or pay raise. You may have been on the receiving end of a toxic culture but allow me to encourage you with the same words that forever changed my life. It's time to produce. *Let 'em know the harvest is coming!*

IT'S. NOT. OVER.

HARVEST IMPLEMENTATION EXERCISE

1. In the left column, list the areas in life where you believe growth is needed.
2. Write how often you actively engage in growth activities in the center column.
3. In the right column, write how often you feel you should be actively engaging in growth activities.

Your responses in frequency should change over time, but for this exercise, answer where you are today. The key is to shorten the gap between what you feel is necessary and what is currently happening.

EXAMPLE

Activity	Actively Engaged	Optimal Engagement
Fitness	2x Week	5x Week
Spiritual	4x Week	Daily
Financial	2x Month	Weekly

CHAPTER 2
The Seed

Have you ever met a person who could not see the immense amount of potential they possessed? It can be frustrating when they don't use what God has given them to make a difference, and you may even be tempted to demand a reason why.

I'm that person. I'm the person who was blinded to my own potential. My mother, Connie Stribling Kuykendall, begged me to see the possibilities life had to offer, to make the right choices, to plant the right seeds. To be fair, very few people have the ability to self-assess and offer an unbiased perspective. We often compare ourselves to others and find ourselves lacking.

Those who live isolated rarely accomplish anything great. We are built to be in community. We grow best when we are surrounded by people who can see past our seed form and identify our potential. To quote a verse from the Bible, "As iron sharpens iron, so one person sharpens another."[1]

If you look back on your life, chances are you could point to at least one person who sharpened you. This may have been rather unpleasant, after all, iron clanging against iron is a loud, violent process. It was my former boss, Ron Gillette, who presented himself as my sharpening tool. He engaged in one of the most direct, heart-to-heart conversations I ever experienced because he recognized I was hurting myself, my teammates and my family.

WE GROW BEST WHEN WE ARE SURROUNDED BY PEOPLE WHO CAN SEE OUR POTENTIAL.

Mr. Gillette was a kind man, an encouraging man. I was a functional addict. Nobody bothered me as long as I was doing my job, and Mr. Gillette could have followed suit, but he didn't. After watching me for quite some time, he pulled me aside and said, "Joe, you have a family and all the potential in the world, but you abuse every opportunity you've been given. I'm watching you waste everything."

He didn't say anything profound. He didn't have a nugget of divine wisdom tucked away for a moment like this. No, he just cared enough to confront me. Maybe it was guilt, maybe it was the fact that he'd experienced life without a father. Either way, he chose not to stand idly by as a witness to my unraveling. He stepped up, aware that this may not end well for him, and spoke truth to a wayward young man.

In that moment he watered my dry, deteriorated seed and brought it back to life. He showed empathy in a way I had never experienced. Brené Brown elaborates on empathy in her book *Daring Greatly*. She writes, "Empathy is a strange and powerful thing. There is no script. There is no right way or wrong way to do it. It's simply listening, holding space, withholding judgment, emotionally connecting, and communicating that incredibly healing message of 'You're not alone.'"[2]

I don't think Mr. Gillette went home and crafted out the perfect argument to deal with my addiction. He saw a young man in need of direction, felt the burden, and decided to do something about it. Years later, after I had turned my life around, I tracked down Mr. Gillette and thanked him for confronting me in my addiction.

Unfortunately six months later, he died of cancer. You may never fully understand the role you play in helping someone else's success seed grow. They may never return to say thank you but do it anyway.

My wife, Damaris, challenged me to be the best husband, father and role model to others. She would never allow me to be less, to remain in seed form. What I had perceived as nagging was really a wife who refused to allow her husband to live a mediocre life. She critiqued my friends, she confronted my choices, and poked the sore spots more than once. She demanded success when I was content with suffering and I'm grateful for that.

All throughout my life the potential was there, but I didn't want to put in the work necessary to produce it. What others saw, I ignored, but I wasn't always this way.

Growing up, even as an at-risk student and product of a single-parent household, I went from being a small-town state championship quarterback and National Honor Society member to receiving a full athletic and academic scholarship at a private college. But I wasted it all away by making excuses and poor choices. A top five biggest mistake I ever made was when I quit football and dropped out of college.

Why did I drop out? Because I wanted to do what was easy. I can't blame anyone other than myself. Instead of using life's changes to fuel me to push harder to achieve my dreams, I used them as an excuse to party and feed my inhibitions.

Over the next 16 years I jumped from one addiction to another. Although I worked full-time and had formed a family, my choices never allowed me to reach the potential I had as an 18-

year-old student-athlete. It wasn't that the potential no longer existed. It was still there. It was just dormant inside of me. Why?

Like a farmer who chooses the right seed to plant, it was my responsibility to know which seeds, or choices, would produce the best harvest. These decisions may come quickly, even intuitively to a lot of people, but for some reason it took devastation to awaken my soul.

We see responsibility avoidance throughout unhealthy organizations. When you are a leader, there will always be someone who thinks they can do your job better than you. Great employees will not look for opportunities to dethrone you, they'll look for ways to balance your weaknesses. Great leaders will understand their shortcomings and surround themselves with great team members.

Poor leaders will mask their weaknesses with intimidation and manipulation. They will pretend to know everything and not succeed at anything. Poor employees will blame their leader for their lack of motivation, direction, or ambition. They will shut down instead of confronting unruly behavior. Poor leaders will create an environment where shutting down and avoiding confrontation is tolerated.

Jocko Willink, author of Extreme Ownership: How U.S. Navy SEALs Lead and Win[3], explains, "Implementing Extreme Ownership requires checking your ego and operating with a high degree of humility. Admitting mistakes, taking ownership, and developing a plan to overcome challenges are integral to any successful team."

When you step into a leadership role you may find yourself cleaning up some messes from your predecessor. You may dismiss all their wins and focus on their losses. You may point to how bad they were in numerous areas but never give them credit for everything they did right. In doing so you'll begin your leadership tenure building on a foundation of dishonor.

Eventually, you'll no longer have to deal with the problems they created. You'll have to deal with the problems you created. Employees who are following your lead and repeat the culture of dishonor you implemented on day one of your leadership journey.

Life is cyclical, leadership is cyclical, and if you lead long enough, you'll reap from the seeds you sow.

As a young man, I was unable to take ownership of my mistakes. In a rented bedroom my lowest point came when I was lying face down perpendicular in a bed. Inside a rented bedroom separated from my wife and children, is where my life jolted in a different direction. It took standing on the edge of total loss before I was able to stop blaming everyone else and take control of my life again.

Seed (The Potential)

Corn seeds may look at tomato seeds and think, I wonder what it's like to be red, slightly plump, and grow on a sturdy vine?

Tomato seeds may admire the corn's potential to grow slim and tall, protected from bugs by a husk and grow silky ponytails. At the end of the day, their potential isn't the same. They will only produce what they're destined to become.

Every person has the ability to produce good fruit. Everyone has great potential. Like seeds, not every person will produce the same thing, but we all have the potential to produce some type of good. By definition, potential is "having or showing the capacity to become or develop into something in the future."

In order to achieve full potential, it requires:

• Belief in the seed's potential
• Placement in the right hands (farmer)
• Planting at the right time (season)
• And in the right environment (soil)

Seed (The Choice)

However, the seed will never fulfill its potential if it's not planted. Every minute, every day we plant seeds. We constantly make choices, some good, some bad. A seed is planted when you choose to:

- Hit the snooze button.
- Consume unhealthy foods.
- Exercise regularly
- Encourage others.
- Embrace people who are different from you.

The results produced are in direct proportion to the choices you make. You cannot discount the power of a single seed's potential to produce, nor can you dismiss a single choice's power to impact.

Small Choices Bring Big Consequences

Consider the small choice of going out to fraternity row and having a few drinks. One drink leads to the next and now you're stumbling back to your dorm room. Struggling to make it up the steps, your intoxicated body collapses in bed — shoes on, lights on and homework unfinished.

The next morning the alarm sounds, you fumble to press the snooze button. Relief! Falling back into a shallow sleep, you're awakened by the repeated knocks on the door. Your hallmate tells you it's 9 a.m. and you've missed your 8 a.m. class.

You wake up frantically and rush to the bathroom to change only to notice out the window your classmates are exiting the building and it's too late. You missed a midterm exam and now your class score drops by two letter grades.

It's at this moment, you have a choice to make. Do you go to the professor and ask if there is anything you can do, or do you disregard any hope of saving face and start drinking again to numb the pain of failure?

You guessed it – I chose drinking.

That was the spring semester of my freshman year at Presbyterian College. I never stopped drinking and scattered bad seed everywhere. It wasn't long before I stopped going to football practice and quit the team. I skipped classes and walked out on my college football dream because one small choice led to bigger choices, and the greater the choice, the greater the impact.

It didn't have to be this way. I had multiple opportunities to stop and salvage the wreckage I had created. But I ran from responsibility instead of towards it.

For the next 16 years, I planted one bad seed after another until I found myself entangled in a life full of weeds.

A garden full of weeds is bad for two reasons. It doesn't produce the life you want and it isn't a place you're proud to call home.

Small choices landed me in places I never thought I'd be. In 2015, I separated from my wife and left my family. I chose the hard road, a road that led me to living out of my car for months. I would pitch a tent in a state park or couch hop. Eventually, I landed in a rented bedroom.

At 3 a.m. on March 16, I'm face down in bed with my shoes on, lights on, and lifework unfinished. I'm too high to go to sleep or get out of bed. I reflected on the life I had produced up to this point. It was depressing. I was in a room surrounded by empty 24 oz. Budweiser cans and a small clear baggie filled with prescription opioids. This wasn't the life I had envisioned for myself. This isn't what I wanted.

I felt empty and alone. Nobody I loved was with me. I could hear the voices in my head from my mom, Mr. Gillette, my wife, and our children. They felt like torturous pleas for me to see and realize my potential, "Wake up, Joe, you have something great on the inside!"

As I wrestled with sleep and the feeling of brokenness, I knew my wife, daughter and son were resting in our house without their husband and father.

Reflecting on my choices as a college freshman, I saw how powerful it was to choose the right seed and plant seeds of expectation and potential. Unlike the moment when my father walked out on our family, I now had a choice, and I chose not to plant bad seed any longer.

"It is not our abilities that show what we truly are. It is our choices." Emphasized the wise wizard Dumbledore to a young Harry Potter. It turns out ability is only a precursor for success. Ability, potential, promise, and love are all intricately tied to the freedom to choose. Without freedom, love could not exist. Without freedom, potential could not be realized.

The trajectory of my adult life stemmed from small choices planted over time. It could be argued it all started from that one reckless night as a college freshman. Each choice compounds to make a person who they are. Some choices rapidly speed up the end result, but all are powerful and determine the direction of your life.

No matter the size of a seed, whatever it produces will be exponentially greater than its genesis. Take an acorn for example. An acorn is less than an inch in circumference but has the potential to produce an oak tree towering more than 70 feet tall. The power of the seed is realized when it's placed in the right hand, at the right time and into the right environment.

The acorn's potential was always there, it just needs the right external factors to bring out its inner potential.

A Sleepy Seed

Mrs. Solomon, my 3rd grade teacher at Buffalo Elementary opened the cabinet door and pulled down a glass jar with dry beans (seeds), sandwich bags, and grabbed a few brown paper towels from the classroom hand washing area.

The class excitedly gathered around grabbing at the bean-filled jar and shaking it to hear the treble sounds as dry beans rattled inside. Mrs. Solomon quickly redirected our attention to the seed lesson.

She explained how the seeds were left over from last year. "Ughhh," we screamed. As if leftover meant old and old meant gross.

"No, class, it's not nasty. The seeds are perfectly fine. They slept all summer inside of Mrs. Solomon's cabinet. And now, it's time to wake them up," Mrs. Solomon softly explained like a compassionate, caring third-grade teacher would.

Pulling out one seed, she asked, "Who wants to wake them up?"

"Ooo, me me, me, me, me, me, me, me!" each child exclaimed with a feverish shaking of one hand, while bouncing on the opposite foot.

"Okay, class, we'll give everyone a chance to help," she assured us.

Then, we took our place around the three rectangle activity tables closest to the cubbies and window as we waited for our sleepy seeds to be delivered.

Mrs. Solomon equally divided the class, distributed the tools, and guided us through the planting activity.

She explained how inside of each seed, there is an "embryo."

"A what?" one little girl asked.

"An embryo. I know, it's a silly word, but it's especially important to know because inside of each seed there is an embryo and it is alive," Mrs. Solomon continued.

"Really?" one boy asked.

"Yes, really," she replied.

"Then, why isn't it growing?" the little boy asked.

"That's our job as farmers. Our job is to wake it up. We do this by giving it what it needs to come alive. Let's wet your paper towel and place the seed inside. Now roll the paper towel like a roly-poly and place it gently inside of the baggie. Once you've done this, place the baggie with your seed inside of the box by the window," she instructed.

This lesson perfectly illustrates a leader's responsibility to his or her team's growth. Each team member's potential is like a sleepy seed. It's living on the inside, but the goal is to awaken their potential.

If you didn't know the embryo lesson, it would be understandable why we see the "dry" outside of someone and forget about what's living on the inside.

Each person is like a seed ready to be planted and grow into something greater than they ever thought possible.

I led a team of sixteen different site managers. I had one manager who many gave up on. She was a veteran leader but her personal struggles smothered a spark of energy, creativity and joy that once shined bright and illuminated the entire organization.

She struggled to find the creative bursts needed to motivate our team. Performing daily operations became a grueling task. There was a sense that we'd soon need to cut ties and fire her. She was, at best, going through the motions. At worst, she called out of work because of night long binges. She was fighting addiction and it was winning.

While many thought her best days were over, I could only think about her potential. Yes, the outside looked lifeless but what if something was still living on the inside, waiting to unfurl its beauty and gifts for all to see?

In reality, every team member has potential to produce. Like a seed, which came from a prosperous, living thing, each person is created to reach their potential and has everything they need to start the growing process.

It's the leader's role to help them see it and to wake it up. Their potential isn't dead, it's just in a dormant stage. While waking this manager's potential was an arduous process, it became one of the most rewarding experiences of my leadership journey. To help another person tap into their potential is better than watching them fade away and waste their gifts.

Would it have been easier to fire her? Yes. Would it have been beneficial to her? Maybe, but probably not. Does grace, empathy, and direction produce loyalty in your team? Yes.

You don't hire great teams, you build them, because everyone comes with a unique set of challenges you will have to address.

There are no guarantees firing this manager would have improved our organization or team. Yes, it would have been easier. But anyone can hire and fire a person. Anyone can go to the grocery store and buy an apple. It takes a leader to see the dormant potential and bring it to life. It takes a farmer who is committed to growing a healthy crop, not just a single tree.

There may be some sleepy seeds in your organization, or you may be that sleepy seed. Maybe you don't see the potential in yourself. There is hope. Here are some tips on how you can "wake up the sleepy seed".

1. Set Clear Expectations.

To be clear is to be kind. Honesty, clarity, and compassion are necessary when setting expectations. Leaders often lean heavily on assumption and their direct reports suffer for it. Unspoken expectations lead to frustration.

Even if the expectations feel lofty or unattainable, your team will be ambitious to reach them if the expectation is coupled with a consistent feedback loop and flexibility to re-evaluate the expectation if it turns out to be unrealistic.

When an individual or team does not reach their potential, it is often because they've taken on an identity that aligns with their organization's expectations. A leader's role is to provide clarity and explain how the team member plays a part in meeting expectations. Communicate early, clearly, honestly, and often, offering the person the best chance to reach their potential.

What do you do when someone is not meeting expectations? You should start by looking in the mirror and asking yourself some very pointed questions. You may ask:

- Did I clearly communicate the expectation or just assume they knew?
- Did I write down the expectation and ensure they understood?
- Did I express how important this expectation is to our culture and company?
- Did they intentionally violate this expectation or was this simply an oversight on their part?
- Did I give them the necessary resources, feedback, and oversight to fulfill this expectation?
- Can I believe the best in them? Can I give them the benefit of the doubt? Was it agreed upon?

Team members rarely set out to be bad teammates. Sure, you may come across some who lack work ethic, are rebellious, disruptive, and foster a toxic environment, but more often than not, bad team members are a result of bad leadership.

Teams don't "get it" as quickly as we think they should. Healthy expectations are repeated and reviewed often. Consistency is key when implementing healthy expectations. If the leader does not follow through, then neither will the employees. It'll be just another suggestion from management and another nail in your proverbial leadership coffin.

When you set expectations, communicate them clearly and often, and provide healthy feedback, your believability will increase and so will your team's trust in your leadership.

If you feel like you've communicated clearly but it's falling on deaf ears, you are not alone. Leadership is a commitment to being misunderstood. If you want to avoid criticism, get out of leadership.

A leader wants to be a great communicator, a motivator, a harborer of passion, the encourager of vision, and an inventor of dreams. A great pursuit such as this does not come without great pestilence. You can minimize the friction if you begin with clear expectations.

2. Listen Empathetically.

According to Simon Sinek, "Empathy is not something we offer to our customers or our employees from nine to five. Empathy is, as Johnny Bravo explains, 'a second by second, minute by minute service that we owe to everyone if we want to call ourselves a leader.' Leadership is not a license to do less; it is a responsibility to do more, and that's the trouble. Leadership takes work. It takes time and energy. The effects are not always easily measured, and they are not always immediate. Leadership is always a commitment to human beings."[4]

Empathy means asking a very simple question and committing to journey wherever that answer would lead. That question is, "Is everything ok?" When we are more committed to results than we are relationships, our minds will often go to the worst place possible. That teammate is not hitting their numbers, they are lagging, they are showing up late, they are going home early. They must be lazy, disinterested, or not want to be employed here.

You may form an airtight narrative and you may be completely wrong.

Helping a seed achieve its potential requires active, empathetic listening. You must listen to their needs and encourage them to see a brighter world. Seek to understand where they are in their personal and professional journey. Asking the right questions will help unpack the unknowns and foster a meaningful relationship. When those relationships exist, growth won't be far behind.

Many choose not to grow as a protective measure and empathetic listening pulls down divisive walls. Listening has the ability to create a better understanding of their behavior styles, past hurts and their personal story. Empathetic listening creates trust, connection, and should be done with a goal to understand versus being understood.

3. Provide Needed Resources and Create Accountability.

Awakening that sleepy seed may require a little extra attention. An unexamined expectation will be an unfulfilled expectation.

Seeds need certain external elements to thrive, and so do team members. Those resources vary, but may require the leader to have more one-on-one conversations than normal, provide outside coaching, or offer incentives.

After you have identified the sleepy seed in your organization, you'll have to ask yourself, "Am I committed or am I just interested?" If you're committed to helping your team awaken their potential, then you will follow through. If you're interested in their growth but not committed, a team member will never produce the high yield needed for organizational growth.

Creating accountability structures, consistent one-on-one oversight meetings, and healthy feedback loops demonstrates your commitment to individual growth and loyalty to the organization's values. Growth only happens when you're held accountable for actions, both good and bad. While it's easier to blame others for your mistakes, authentic progress occurs when you own the situation, move towards finding solutions and take action.[5]

Small Seeds, Big Production

When I planted my first organic, raised bed vegetable garden, I knew extraordinarily little about growing food other than it required seed, good soil, water, and the appropriate season.

I learned two lessons rather quickly. A tiny seed can grow into something big, and each plant matures on their own unique timeline.

A bibb lettuce seed is about the size of the letter "I" you see here on the page. Due to its minuscule nature and my large hands, I dropped more lettuce seeds than intended. Each black speck was lost in the rich, compost-filled soil, so I let nature do what nature does.

Now mind you, I started with less than ¼ of the seeds inside the packet. What grew in the garden box shocked my amateur gardener mind. Less than two weeks passed and there were scores of tiny, vibrant green sprouts showing their heads. I ran inside to get my wife to show her. She was amazed and said, "I hope you like lettuce."

We knew we'd give much of it way because saving harvested lettuce by traditional preservation methods isn't possible, and there's only so much lettuce one family can consume before it wilts.

How could this small amount of seed create more food than one family could eat?

Easy, seeds are created for growth and production. It's the only thing they know how to do. I used to think smaller seeds produced smaller things, but now I know seed size doesn't dictate the final product.

Have you worked for a leader who couldn't see the potential in you? In others? Their leadership blindness prevented the team members potential, as well as the organization's potential from being realized.

Every seed has potential, but if a farmer refuses to acknowledge the potential and commit to developing the seed, he will never receive all the seed could offer.

Leadership requires a sixth sense, an ability to see possibilities in the most unlikely places or people. There are acorns in every organization. Unleashing the potential inside of someone requires flexibility and a commitment to adapt to their story. A leader may need to remove old ways of thinking, old business models, or archaic expectations to reach that person.

Controlling your thought life is crucial for any leader or team member. It is healthy to identify the detractors on the team. What are the existing thought patterns that are limiting the organization's growth? Leaders must ask themselves:

- What am I missing?
- Who has the potential to grow but hasn't been given a chance? Who has failed and now needs a second chance?
- How can I help team members see their potential?

To see the big potential inside of a small seed is the missing link between average results and a bountiful harvest.

Visionary leaders have an exceptional ability to find the bleakest opportunities and turn them into the most profitable and sustainable acts.

Every farmer has a choice to make. They can either see the seed's potential and bring it to life or let it sit in a glass jar for someone else to cultivate.

How disappointing to know there was an oak tree inside your organization waiting to grow but you never helped them produce their potential?

VISIONARY LEADERS HAVE THE EXCEPTIONAL ABILITY TO TURN BLEAK OPPORTUNITIES INTO PROFITABLE AND SUSTAINABLE ACTS.

An organization's continued growth depends on leadership and their ability to extract potential from team members. Each extraction produces new life and opportunity. A seed, like other living organisms, has a living component. Yes, even a dry seed inside of your favorite box store is alive. It has all the potential to sprout, grow, and produce but it needs a sower, soil, and the right season to come alive.

"A small seed has the power to break through a crushing rock, bloom from a city sidewalk crack, or produce after years of neglect on an abandoned barn floor. And so do you." - Joe Pettit

HARVEST IMPLEMENTATION EXERCISE

Identify your top two gifts or potential growth areas — personally or professionally. Write them in the space below.

Gift #1 _____

Gift #2 _____

Personal Growth Area #1 _____

Personal Growth Area #2 _____

Professional Growth Area #1 _____

Professional Growth Area #2 _____

If you're struggling to identify them, answer this question: What do others tell you about your gifts? Knowing this will ease the process of waking your sleeping potential so you can produce results.

The hardest part but the most important step is to pinpoint unseen potential inside of you. Trust your intuition and write down what you believe can occur if seed goes from a dormant stage to a living thing.

Let 'em know the harvest is coming.

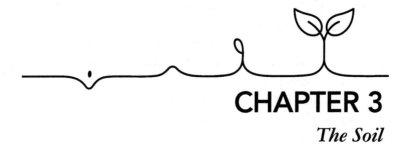

CHAPTER 3
The Soil

"You can have all the right strategy in the world; if you don't have the right culture, you're dead." - Patrick Whitesell

As important a seed is for growth, the seed's environment can taint or promote its potential.

I had the great fortune of growing up in Union County, South Carolina for the first 18 years of my life. Union enjoyed nearly a century of booming textile jobs that employed many residents including many of my family members. My mother was a seamstress and ran the "cloth shop" located at Buffalo Mill before transferring to manage payroll operations. When Buffalo Mill closed its doors, my single mother was laid off but had the opportunity to continue her education. She later earned her associate's degree despite the current economic and family battles.

Against all odds, my mother invested in me and did her best to place me in a growth environment. She is still my number one supporter and encouraged me to be the best in everything I did.

The culture my Mom created was based on a few core values and beliefs — education, community, kindness, and finding purpose in life.

She modeled each one and this created a growth environment, but she had to fight daily to ensure the environment stayed steady. As a young boy I didn't know the sacrifices she made, the sleepless nights, or the constant worry, wondering if she was doing the right thing. Yet in her core she knew if she could give good soil, the seed would take care of the rest. If she could build a healthy home environment despite outside influences, her boys would have a chance to succeed.

According to the National Fatherhood Initiative, a child who is raised in a father-absent home is affected in the following ways:[1]

- 4x Greater Risk of Poverty
- More Likely to Have Behavior Problems
- 2x Greater Risk of Infant Mortality
- More Likely to Go to Prison
- More Likely to Commit Crime
- 7x More Likely to Become Pregnant as a Teen
- More Likely to Face Abuse and Neglect
- More Likely to Abuse Drugs and Alcohol
- 2x More Likely to Suffer Obesity
- 2x More Likely to Drop Out of School

My mother didn't know these statistics when she was raising my me and my brothers. She didn't have to. She was prepared to pick up the slack and do everything she could to foster a growth environment. She made the hard choices and refused to quit. She sacrificed her own comfort and convenience to help nurture my personal growth.

Like a sustainable farmer, my mother knew "life soil" was her best investment. Soil contains everything a seed needs to grow. It provides an environment for growth but not all soils are the same.

For example, grounds surrounding an old chemical plant contain deadly deposits that contaminate and kill a seed's potential. The chemicals in the soil could also produce fruit that could make an animal or person ill. The soil needs to be tested, amended, and new soil must be added so that the seed receives the correct amount of nutrients for a healthy yield.

Bad soil can destroy a seed's potential, but healthy soil encourages growth.

A sustainable farmer takes a strategic approach to soil management. They understand a healthy soil promotes a high yield and helps manage internal and external opposition. They work hard developing healthy soils. They know when you incorporate healthy soil with the proper nutrients, over time it will result in a higher yield and more resilient plants, which will be able to compete with insects, diseases, and uncontrollable weather conditions.

The same is true with workplace culture. Many corporate environments are toxic. According to a 2022 article published by Bloomberg, an analysis of more than 1.4 million Glassdoor reviews for companies across 38 industries found that company culture is 12.4 times more likely than compensation to predict whether an employee leaves. This held true for workers in both front-line and so-called knowledge worker jobs.

WORKPLACE CULTURE REQUIRES SPECIAL EXAMINATION AND TACTICS TO TEST ITS HEALTH AND VITALITY.

The challenging part about amending and correcting workplace culture, like soil, is that it's unseen. Often unhealthy cultures look like thriving ones until growth stops or people burnout.

Workplace culture requires special examination and tactics to test its health and vitality.

Simon Sinek says leaders must ask "How do I create an environment where people work their natural best?"[2]

A healthy workplace culture is not a single entity. It is a combination of values, empathy, and positive intention. Companies often possess three key ingredients to maintaining employee engagement and low turnover.

1. Opportunity for Advancement

Nobody has ever expressed excitement for being in a "dead-end job". A dead-end job is a job where the employee is "perceived" to have reached the peak of their potential. Perceived, not proven. Personality differences, preference, or past conflicts may cause a leader to distance themselves from an employee.

Instead of nurturing the seed they ignore it, placing them in a no-win situation. For the employer, it is a self-fulfilling prophecy. They will highlight the worst attributes of an individual, disregard their best attributes, and use their leverage to ensure they never promote beyond their current status.

In a healthy organization not only are employees nurtured, they are also given a clear sightline for advancement. Not every employee may advance to the same position, but the options are at least clear and attainable. Then an employee is equipped with the information necessary to determine whether or not they can advance their career elsewhere. It won't be because they weren't nurtured, it will be because they were nurtured and equipped to thrive in their industry, even if that means it's with another company. According to the Harvard Business Review:[3]

> A survey of over 400,000 U.S. workers found that when people
> believe promotions are managed effectively, they're more than
> twice as likely to give extra effort at work and to plan a long-

term future with their company. They are also five times as likely to believe leaders act with integrity.

However, if promotions aren't managed well, one person's success can foster feelings of resentment in others, and the career aspirations of employees across the company can be left unrealized.

To improve how your team feels about promotions, make sure you have conversations with people about their aspirations before a new role even opens up. And when there is a promotion opportunity available, encourage people to apply — don't wait for them to put up their hand. Finally, once a decision has been made, be transparent about why the person who got it deserved it.

Yet, opportunity for advancement isn't the only reason people stay committed to an organization.

2. Proper Compensation

Proper compensation comes in many forms. Employees long to be respected and rewarded for their work. This may mean added incentives for a job well done, higher than standard pay, or even public recognition. When an employee feels valued, they will respond with loyalty and an organization's turnover rate will reduce.

If an organization wants to keep plants rooted in their garden, they best make sure they are offering the seed excellent soil. Studying the market value for a position, meeting the external needs of an employee, and honoring their time with their family all add to fostering a sustainable and satisfying work environment.

Some companies go above and beyond offering additional incentives like a gym membership, paid paternal and maternal leave, tuition reimbursement, and extra time off. In the long run, many of these incentives more than pay for themselves.

According to Gallup, "Losing your best people means losing your reliable winners, your constant innovators, and your most effective problem solvers. Internally, it breaks down team morale. Externally, it can mean lost customer relationships. Depending on the quality of the exit, it can threaten your brand or, at worst, lead to litigation."[4]

Gallup proceeds to explain that the loss of an employee can cost a business one-half to two times the employee's annual salary. Yet, companies still clinch their fists when it comes to give incentives. A $10 a month employee gym membership doesn't seem like a waste when it saves you over $100,000 and allows you to retain your top talent.

3. Healthy Oversight

Listen, you could get paid well, receive all kinds of perks, and have a clear path for advancement but still be absolutely miserable at your place of employment. In the end, it's all about people. It's about the people you serve and the people who you report to. For

BEING A **GOOD LEADER** HAS NOTHING TO DO WITH YOUR **POSITION**. IT HAS EVERYTHING TO DO WITH YOU AS A **PERSON**.

many, if your boss makes your life miserable it won't matter how much they pay you or how many gym memberships they throw your way. You. Will. Leave.

People want to be financially stable, but even more so, they want to be mentally, emotionally, and relationally cared for by their employers. If your work relationships are creating stress at home, causing you to miss important family moments, or affecting your physical health, you'll not stay long.

Being a good leader has nothing to do with your position. It has everything to do with you as a person. Great bosses:[5]

- Foster social connections
- Show empathy
- Go out of their way to help
- Encourage people to talk about their problems

How do you know if you are seeded in healthy soil? You need to test it.

Testing The Soil

The Great Resignation that happened post COVID-19 has allowed many employees to evaluate where they spend their time, which is important considering we spend an estimated one-third of our lives working. Through the recent pandemic, employees re-prioritized their lives, many taking pay cuts if it meant greater fulfillment at home.

Those who switched jobs became a great deal more concerned with a healthy, positive work culture than with perks and pay.

"Global jobs website Glassdoor surveyed more than 5,000 adults in the U.S., the U.K., France and Germany throughout June to determine their priorities when it came to job satisfaction. According to the study, 56% of workers ranked a strong workplace culture as more important than salary, with more than three-in-four workers saying they'd consider a company's culture before applying for a job there."[6]

An experienced farmer knows a healthy harvest comes from healthy soil so prior to planting they test soil fertility.

Just because a corn farmer has successfully planted and grown high yielding crops doesn't mean a new land automatically generates equal results. Taking a soil assessment is vital to determine if the soil is healthy. Some soils require additives, some need toxins and chemicals removed, much like a place of employment. Removing toxic employees who refuse to grow is just as important as adding healthy employees.

According to Penn State Extension, "A soil test provides very important information about nutrient levels in the soil."

Farmers are primarily concerned with three nutrients and matter found in soil — nitrogen (N), phosphorus (P), and potassium (K).

- Nitrogen (N) is largely responsible for the growth of leaves on the plant.
- Phosphorus (P) is largely responsible for root growth and flower and fruit development.
- Potassium (K) helps the overall functions of the plant perform correctly.

Soil sampling provides a farmer with valuable information that cannot be detected by simply looking at the dirt. A soil sample must be tested to gain an accurate diagnosis. Once a farmer understands what's inside of the soil, steps can be taken to choose the best plants and know how to move forward with soil management.

Leaders must also take specific steps when considering the health of their workplace culture. Many organizations struggle to recruit or retain top talent because workplace culture is toxic or unhealthy.

If soil needs appropriate balances of NPK, workplace cultures need ideal nutrient levels as well. There are a multitude of workplace culture components that will enhance productivity, happiness, and profits.

Let's look at the three workplace essentials needed to ensure sustainable, profitable growth: Learning Culture, Kindness Culture and a Purpose-Linked Culture (L-K-P).

When one part is off, people and projects will not produce to their fullest potential. Upon assessing the workplace culture, deficiencies will highlight which areas are in need of improvement.

Learning Culture (L-K-P)

Most people wish they had more time and money. What if there is a way to create more time and money?
Creating a culture centered on learning will not put 25 hours in a day or make you rich overnight, but it will create opportunities where you can make better use of your time and money.

Leaders who create an environment of continuous learning build a living organism where people have ample growth opportunities, embrace change and are more engaged at work.

Studies show that the number one perk millennials want at work is growth and development. As just one example, here's the results of a study reported in Mary Meeker's Internet Trends report:

> Organizations intentionally investing in their current team members design a proactive plan for retention and external threats. They develop a leadership pipeline and encourage advancement. Leaders must not see a learning culture as an expense but as an investment. It is a way to show, not tell your team members you value them.

A learning culture consists of three main components: training, coaching, and mentoring (T-C-M). Each one is significantly different, but all promote growth and aid the ability to reach their full potential. Healthy cultures create space for all three.

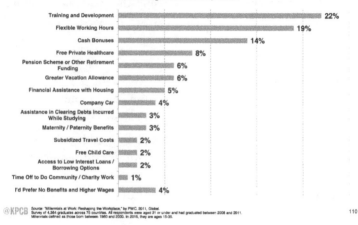

Millennials' Most Valued Work Benefits =
1) Training & Development 2) Flexible Hours 3) Cash Bonuses

Which Three Benefits Would You Most Value From an Employer?
% Ranking Each 1st Place, Global

Benefit	%
Training and Development	22%
Flexible Working Hours	19%
Cash Bonuses	14%
Free Private Healthcare	8%
Pension Scheme or Other Retirement Funding	6%
Greater Vacation Allowance	6%
Financial Assistance with Housing	5%
Company Car	4%
Assistance in Clearing Debts Incurred While Studying	3%
Maternity / Paternity Benefits	3%
Subsidized Travel Costs	2%
Free Child Care	2%
Access to Low Interest Loans / Borrowing Options	2%
Time Off to Do Community / Charity Work	1%
I'd Prefer No Benefits and Higher Wages	4%

@KPCB Source: "Millennials at Work: Reshaping the Workplace," by PWC, 2011, Global.
Survey of 4,364 graduates across 75 countries. All respondents were aged 31 or under and had graduated between 2008 and 2011.
Millennials defined as those born between 1980 and 2000. In 2015, they are ages 15-35.   110

While they're similar, there are distinct differences as well. Let's take a closer look at each of these.

Training

Training, typically, focuses on knowledge transfer. It is how team members grow their understanding of current systems or processes, or acquire and develop new skills. Examples include webinars, conferences, and self-paced online programs.

Training should be purposeful, delivered consistently, and align with individual and/or organizational goals.

Training and development programs are offered in four primary areas: new hires, job-specific training, personal development, and upskilling. Each provides a different competitive advantage, but all encourage growth.

Coaching

While coaching and mentoring can overlap, one of the distinct differences is that a coach aims to guide a team member more than advise them. Coaching is commonly accomplished through one-on-one meetings, and involves an individualized plan focused on growth towards business and personal goals.

Coaching is not exclusive to Fortune 500 executives. It is an accessible opportunity for organizations looking to promote a growth culture. As a leader, you engage team members by meeting them where they are to take them to where you believe they can go.

Mentoring

"A mentor pulls you to where they are, while a coach pushes you to where they believe you can be." C.L. "Shep" Shepherd

The workplace is changing so much that employers are requiring rapid skill development to keep up with the digital age. A typical employee today has more access to training and resources than they have time to take advantage of. Therefore, it is essential for companies to implement a mentoring program. Mentors can help workers gain the skills they need to succeed, and this in turn allows the company to grow.

There are many benefits of mentoring at the workplace, including:

- Increased productivity
- Retention of top talent
- Better communication skills

Mentoring programs allow employees to learn from experienced workers in all aspects of their job, including management skills, effective sales techniques, and public speaking. The mentor-mentee relationship also encourages networking and gives workers support and a safety net when needed.

A study by Forbes found that mentees were promoted more than their non-mentored peers because mentors gave them opportunities for growth and motivated them to reach new heights. Additionally, since mentees learn from experienced workers instead of relying on textbook learning, they are able to retain what they learned more effectively than someone who just read about it in a book or manual.[7]

Mentoring is more than meeting with another person, it's an opportunity to create tangible change.

A mid-level leader in the aerospace industry recently shared in an interview how participating in his company's mentoring program profited the company and his family. Below is an excerpt from our conversation.

"When I worked as a global leader in the aerospace industry, it was my responsibility to ensure another department had a product on hand so that I could issue it to another department. My first year there I was learning the ropes kind of identifying how things worked and how to use the ordering systems and the cadence of ordering. Going into my second year I had a groove as I followed internal processes and ordering things consistently ensuring things ran smoothly.

However my leadership growth became stagnant and honestly, I became complacent and wasn't giving my all. After feeling unmotivated and disengaged, I realized something needed to change.

I signed up for our company's mentoring and leadership growth program where I was matched with an individual who not only met with me but showed interest in my potential as a leader and as a person. He helped me get the necessary skills to be better and to give more effort.

He sparked change and I increased my productivity level and became more engaged in the organization's goals.

For the year, the site was averaging $1.43 million dollars in spending on hazardous material. After going through the leadership training and mentoring, I was able to ask questions in a one-on-one mentor setting and found answers that would bring an additional $750,000 profit to the company.

His mentoring forced me to look at ways to cut costs, identify materials specs, and to connect with material suppliers who could help be more efficient and profitable.

I received an award for my efforts and gained a promotion. Without the company's mentoring and leadership training, I would not have been provided the tools to do this and I never would have met the gentleman that helped facilitate my personal and professional growth.

Training, coaching, and mentoring are the antithesis of complacency. If you're not growing, you're dying.

Organizations who ignore any one of these growth opportunities are writing their bottom line obituary and losing team members to organizations focused on growth and development. While losing team members is a big concern, keeping disengaged team members is even more alarming.

According to research by Gallup, "17.2% of an organization's employees are disengaged. Each disengaged employee costs organizations 34% in productivity per year."[8]

For example, if Robert is a disengaged employee at ABC Capital earning $50,000 per year. He is costing your ABC Capital $17,000 per year in loss profits due to lack of productivity.

If ABC Capital employs 100 people, take Robert's $17,000 and multiply it by 17 and you will see the price of a disengaged employee ($289,000 of lost productivity).

Training, coaching and mentoring (T-C-M) can be the answer to disengaged employees and strengthen the organization's culture. High performance requires an investment. Thriving organizations see it as an investment and the number one tool for sustainable growth.

Assessing your organization for training, coaching and mentoring is the first step to producing growth and maximizing its full potential. T-C-M adds nutrients to strengthen workplace soil.

Kindness (L-K-P)

As a product of a small South Carolina town called Buffalo, kindness was embedded into our cultural DNA. Southern manners were non-negotiable. From a young age my mother taught me how to be kind, show respect to others, and always say "yes, sir," "no, sir," "yes, ma'am," and "no, ma'am". She taught me to appreciate, embrace, and celebrate the differences of others.

My mother, along with my grandparents, modeled that you can always choose to be kind to others. I later learned not everyone is taught these principles, nor understands the importance of kindness. I did recognize, those who showed kindness seemed happier, more peaceful and willing to help a friend, family member, or even a stranger.

It is equally important to show kindness in the workplace as it is in our personal lives.

Team members demonstrating kindness are more engaged, caring, and improve morale for others. Not only does kindness create better relationships, which is good for any culture, but it also makes people happier.

Happiness has also been shown to improve productivity and increased productivity is good for growth. Research from the University of Warwick revealed that happy people are 12 percent more productive at work than unhappy people.[9]

Kindness is an essential part of any vibrant work environment. It is the unseen characteristic that affects worker productivity and job satisfaction, which is the glue that holds an organization together during challenging times. It's also the *secret ingredient* to help a team member see their potential and encourage growth.

A commitment to being kind can bring many important benefits to any organization. Verbally acknowledging contributions and encouraging others are two of many vital components to build a kind work environment. *What gets recognized gets repeated.*

Showing appreciation openly acknowledges their contributions and worth. It engages team members by affirming their value and tying their work to the organization's mission.

According to Dr. Paul White, co-author of The New York Times bestseller The 5 Languages of Appreciation in the Workplace, words of affirmation are the primary way employees like to be shown appreciation in the workplace. Not money, not doughnuts in the break room — although there is a time and place for that — but simple words of affirmation is what team members desire.

Below are two examples of offering words of affirmation and building kindness in the workplace.

1. "I can't tell you how much it means to our organization that you were willing to pause your current project to help onboard new interns. You were willing to temporarily sacrifice your progress to show hospitality to our newest team mem-

ber and truly live out our mission — 'show kindness at all times, at all costs'. We are better because of you. Thank you!"

2. "I know having a report thrown at you at the last minute isn't ideal. You took it on with grace and the presentation was a huge success. Your support and willingness to do this without complaining is what makes our organization thrive. You have a rare talent that I and our entire leadership team admires. We are better because of you. Thank you!"

Encouraging Others

Open, verbal acknowledgement of individual and team contributions are critical to boosting employee morale and keeping them motivated. While similar, there is one distinct difference I'd like to highlight between open acknowledgement and encouragement.

As mentioned earlier in this chapter, words of affirmation are what a person receives when they succeed at a task. Encouragement is what a person needs to push through adversity to reach success.

ENCOURAGEMENT IS A HEART EXCHANGE.

When encouragement is present in the workplace, you'll find team members who are willing to collaborate, sacrifice, and go all-in towards the organization's mission.

Encouragement is a heart exchange. It gives an individual what they lack to persevere, grow and accomplish more than ever imagined. For example, if you want to encourage basil plants in your garden, you've got to water them. In this instance, water is the missing ingredient. When the farmer pours water on the basil plant, they are giving what they have to strengthen its development.

If you want to encourage your team members, you express support of their dreams and career goals to promote engagement and growth. Leaders have accessibility and resources to strengthen their team's growth. They must first decide to plant the seed of encouragement.

To better illustrate this principle, let's break down the word, encourage. The prefix en means to "put into". The word courage is a Latin derivative of "cor" which means "heart." It is where we get the Spanish word for heart, corazon.

Courage, according to Google Dictionary, is "the ability to do something that frightens one." Another definition is "strength in the face of pain or grief."

A constant exchange of bravery and resilience from one person to another occurs in a culture of encouragement. It happens when a team member sees a colleague lacking self-confidence or fighting to overcome adversity and expresses empathy. They take the initiative to step in and encourage, acknowledging what's missing and offering to help fill the void.

Fostering a work culture where encouragement is commonplace builds resilience, loyalty, confidence. Employees feel supported by their co-workers and bosses, and they are quick to support others, reciprocating what they've received.

Acts of kindness can be revealed in various forms, like a handwritten thank you card, welcoming a new colleague by inviting them to coffee or lunch, or showing sincere, yet appropriate concern for their personal life.

While kindness in the workplace can be considered weakness, it's actually the catalyst for profitable, sustainable growth. Strategy requires a healthy culture to bloom to its full potential.

Open to Team Feedback

Employee engagement and the ability to listen are gaining traction in leadership circles, and it's hard to believe that it needs repeating.

Team members want to be heard because when they're heard they feel valued. When they feel valued, they're more loyal and engaged at work.

At the end of the day, they want to know you care and there is no better way to show that than by creating space to listen.

But listening isn't enough. You must show you are listening by practicing active and empathetic listening.

Active listening is the art of listening and watching nonverbal cues and responding to confirm you understand. Demonstrating concern while your team member speaks, builds rapport and deepens your connection with them. Your openness to team input demands leadership humility and humility breeds trust.

Imagine a culture where workers try to outdo one another with kind acts and demonstrate grace, encouragement, and empathy for others.

Another way leaders can create a healthy work culture and demonstrate consideration for others is to provide clear communication that connects team members' purposes with the organization's mission.

Purpose-Linked Culture (L-K-P)

Clear communication means connecting people and their purpose to organizational goals.

Clarity isn't just an ideal culture component, it is an absolute necessity. According to a report from the Economist Intelligence Unit,[9] poor communication can lead to low morale, missed performance goals and even lost sales.

The top two reasons for poor communication found by the Economist Intelligence Unit's report were "different communication styles" and "unclear responsibilities." Effective communication can be the competitive advantage an organization needs to create a healthy work culture.

Different communication styles present a multitude of challenges. A communicator makes assumptions based on their own natural communication preferences and has difficulty seeing why a connection isn't happening. It can also happen when traditional thinking prevents adaptation and implementation of new concepts or processes. The best communicators know how to adapt their communication to different situations and audiences. A great communicator understands to create a healthy work culture you must change your approach depending on the person and situation.

For generations, fathers have taught their children how to fish. So, when my son was around 12 years old, I took him fishing. Now this wasn't our first fishing experience together, but it was the first time my sole intention was to teach him how to fish.

There was only one problem; I didn't know how to fish. Let me clarify, I understand the concept of fishing and know the basics like rod and reel, hook, bait, cast, and eat. But a basic understanding is all I have and that's okay when teaching a newbie.

We went to the store and purchased the appropriate bait to catch our intended fish, two rods and reels, a pack of hooks, and two five-gallon buckets.

Everyone needs a five-gallon bucket. It's the dual-purpose instrument that serves as a seat and then as a holding place for all the fish you'll catch.

It was a perfect Charleston summer evening and the pond we visited wasn't too crowded. We took out the bait, placed it on the hook, and cast the weighted line into the middle of the water. As the bait sank into the water, we took a seat on the upside-down plastic bucket. Slowly reeling in the line, we anxiously waited for the one — the mammoth fish — to grab our bait and the game would finally begin between fish and fisherman.

I had envisioned media crews clamoring to take a photo of our record catch. Surely, we would be in the newspaper the next day as we snagged the catch of a lifetime. Our pictures would immediately go viral, and we would be instafamous.

Unfortunately, the big moment never happened. With each cast, our hook came back with a branch or algae bumming a ride to the shore. The feelings of failure grew each time we reeled in our hooks. The only thing we were successful with was losing our bait or cleaning debris from the pond. We were unable to successfully catch any fish.

Thinking we may be in the wrong spot, I looked up to see where others were having success.

My attention darted towards two guys making noise across the water as they reeled in one fish after another.

I wasn't surprised someone else was catching more fish than us. My failure had dished out a heavy dose of humble pie. I tried to teach my son a lesson I hadn't learned, and I came up empty. Aside from their vivacious energy, I noticed only one guy had a rod and reel. The other played the role of "hype man," like an emcee does before the main act takes the stage.

The lead man cast the fishing line parallel with the embankment and within seconds he'd catch a fish, passing his caught fish towards his partner who stood behind him. His partner would take the fish off and bait the hook again.

They continued their unique casting parallel with the embankment versus my traditional method of casting to the middle of deeper waters.

I was puzzled. I didn't understand his approach, but it worked. My son and I left that day with empty five-gallon buckets, and a lesson about fishing and about life.

In order to catch fish, you may have to discard old thinking and change your approach.

The same is true with workplace communication. If you're going to have a successful work culture, you must change your approach when communicating with others. Your approach may need to be altered several times during one day and thousands of times over the course of one project to create a work environment that breeds respect, clarity and connection.

For example, perhaps one team member prefers to lead conversations with small talk laced with personable stories in an attempt to connect with the person before discussing a task. Their preferred communication style tends to be more of a gregarious and interactive style, or "high I" according to Dr. William Marston's DISC theory.

However, another person may focus primarily on the task at hand and how to obtain fast results. Their idea of effective communication is to solve problems and then have small talk.

If you're not familiar with different behavior types and how each prefers to communicate, misunderstandings and unnecessary conflict will arise. One way to solve this is to develop a culture of human behavior knowledge.

Self-awareness is critical to success and likewise, self-management is pivotal to leadership and workplace culture transformation.

If you're interested in learning more about human behavior and your personal communication preferences, scan the QR code above to complete a human behavior assessment. The customized and detailed report will provide insight you can use to strengthen self-awareness and understand how to operate in your true talents and gifts.

If you're interested in a live coaching call debrief or group training with one of our certified team members, click to see availability inside of the link. Taking this step can be the difference between a one-off season of success and a lifetime of achievement.

Purpose, Words, and Action

Purpose is found in a leader's words and actions. Clear communication is vital because it provides a bridge from team member to purpose. Connecting a team member's value and contribution to the organization is vital to sustained team motivation, drive, and resilience. When communication is clear and values are engrained, the organization will have what it needs to persevere through good times and bad.

Purpose is in the seed but a leader's ability to consistently communicate the why behind each who and what promotes an environment where potential can be reached.

Where there is clear communication connecting a team member's purpose with the mission, you will find an unstoppable force. It is a place where growth happens naturally and more abundantly, a place where the people inside the organization can combat internal and external opposition that often eradicates other teams.

Knowing your soil is key to understanding how to care for a seed, how to best determine which plants will thrive in the environment and what needs to be removed or added to the soil.

I once thought if the strategy was good, the result was certain. I was wrong. Without healthy soil, without healthy culture, the best ideas will never come to fruition. If the soil is not ready to receive the seed, it doesn't matter how great the seed is. It doesn't matter how big it should grow.

High expectations without proper cultivation will lead to organizational failure. You can hope, pray, or dream of a healthy business, but unless you put in the time, care, and attention needed to prepare the soil (environment), tend to the threats (toxic behavior), and care for the plants (employees), you'll never achieve the desired harvest.

During my career as a school nutrition administrator, overseeing multiple schools, I was presented with an opportunity to start fresh, to try something never done before. We didn't have a formal training program in our organization, but we did recognize the importance of installing a complete program directed towards developing new leadership, existing team members, and onboarding new hires.

We identified the benefits, persons responsible, and how it would benefit operations. There was a plan. It was not a perfect one, but there was enough to get the plane off the ground and continue building. Then came the pushback. Employees expressed concern about how the changes would impact operations. Many questioned how realistic the expectations were as they attempted to balance new year challenges while training new hires. This was a brand-new concept within the organization, so hesitation was expected.

When change happens, whether at home or at work, we all internally ask one question. "What does this mean for me?"

One accommodation led to another until it compromised the training program goals and allowed current work environment conditions to win out.

We failed to acknowledge that our work culture — our shared belief and values — would not be prepared to embrace a new training program because it was a foreign concept and our department had not been a learning culture in the past. The implementation strategy existed, but we missed a key component; an environment focused more on learning than short-term production.

We became focused on short-term production and forgot to add the needed nutrients back into the work environment. Specifically, we lacked a culture with emphasis on ongoing T-C-M. Eventually, the training program stalled due to a pandemic but has taken off again with a new focus geared towards training and development.

I learned to focus more on the culture before tackling the next big idea or project. It would've been advantageous to slowly deposit a learning culture into the organization as opposed to a heavy dose all at once. Yes, team culture needs a learning environment, but we needed to address the things depleting the environment first. It would've been beneficial to add doses of clear communication highlighting a learning environment and how it would create a happier workplace. Instead, we proceeded without proactive communication, failed to gain momentum and never hit the tipping point author Malcolm Gladwell explains as "that magic moment when an idea, trend, or social behavior crosses a threshold, tips and spreads like wildfire."[10]

Without the proper soil, plants will not produce their full potential. The stronger a soil, the better its capacity to fight insects, diseases, and equip plants to grow despite uncontrollable weather conditions.

Likewise, workplace environments missing the key components will not thrive. Team members will be overcome by uncontrollable, external forces like a global pandemic, market turns or supply chain issues. The stronger a workplace culture, the better it can withstand the harsh outside conditions and protect its greatest assets — its people and its profits.

We will discuss more tactful ways to "prep" the soil later in the book but know that the proper workplace environments need constant attention in the beginning. As time passes and more healthy deposits are made to the environment, the culture will begin to protect attacks and promote organic growth. The result will be a shared responsibility to protect and nurture the culture. While the leader may sow the seed, the rest of the team will water and protect the harvest.

It is the responsibility of a leader to periodically check on the work environment and assess its health and effectiveness. The goal is to develop a vibrant and alive work culture where team members are happy, productive, and resilient. The healthier the soil, the better chance of sustainable growth over time.

HARVEST IMPLEMENTATION EXERCISE
The Workplace Soil Assessment

In this chapter, we identified the importance of a healthy work environment so team members have the best chance to grow and produce.

Like soil that needs three main nutrients for a seed to have optimal growth, healthy work environments supporting optimal growth need three main things as well — a learning culture, kindness, and clear communication connecting people's purpose with the organizational mission. In addition to the three main nutrients mentioned in this chapter, there are many more vital components of a workplace culture.

What would you add to create a healthy work soil?

In the spaces below, add your work environment essentials. Once you have an updated list, I challenge you to take "The Workplace Soil Assessment."

The activity consists of three separate reflection exercises, depending on your organizational structure, and will require a couple of hours. There are opportunities to reflect individually, with leadership members only and with frontline team members.

1. **Individually**
   a. Add your success soil essentials to the list below first. (Author's Note: I separated T-C-M because it is three separate essentials to a learning culture.)
   b. Answer the following questions in private. The goal is to answer openly and honestly regarding your organization's work environment without being swayed by others.
   c. Reflect on the healthy work environment terms, answer how frequently you observe them, and list specific notes in the right column.
   d. Be sure notes include tangible examples of how you have seen this in action. If you can't remember a specific example or have seen it all, write, "Not Observed."

Place the Corresponding Number Next to the Activity

1 - Once a Week
2 - More Than Once a Week
3 - Once a Month
4 - Once a Quarter
5 - Once a year
6 - Never
7 - Other

Activity	Frequency
Training	
Mentoring	
Coaching	
Kindness	
Purpose-Linked Communication	

2. Leadership
   a. Have your team read the entire chapter.
   b. Add your work environment essentials first to the list below.
   c. Answer the following questions individually before your team. The goal is to answer openly and honestly regarding your organization's work environment without being swayed by others.
   d. Reflect on the healthy work environment terms, answer how frequently you observe them and list specific notes in the right column.
   e. Be sure notes include tangible examples of how you have seen this in action. If you can't remember a specific example or have seen it all, write, "Not Observed."

3. Frontline Team Members
   a. Have your frontline team leaders read the entire chapter.
   b. Add your work environment essentials to the list below first.
   c. Answer the following questions individually first. The goal is to answer openly and honestly regarding your organization's work environment without being swayed by others.
   d. Reflect on the healthy work environment terms, answer how frequently you observe them, and list specific notes in the right column.
   e. Be sure notes include tangible examples of how you have seen this in action. If you can't remember a specific example or have seen it all, write, "Not Observed."

CHAPTER 4
The Farmer

S
o far, we've discussed the power of a seed and how it's comparable to the potential found in each team member. We've unpacked ways to bring a seed to life; it requires soil management to prepare the healthiest workplace culture to achieve optimal productivity and promote job satisfaction for team members.

Before we move forward discussing the role of a farmer, it's important to have a working definition of a farmer. A farmer is a person who cultivates land or crops or raises animals. For the sake of this book, we're looking at it from the standpoint of a farmer who cultivates land or crops.

Every farmer has the responsibility to cultivate. When a farmer cultivates, he or she prepares land for crops or gardening. Another definition is to try to acquire or develop a quality, sentiment or skill.

An organization's goal is to bring goods or services to market, but the primary responsibility of a leader is to prepare team members for success personally and professionally. The best leaders cultivate high yields, not by accident, but with intentional investing and developing their team's skills and performance.

Before you can develop others, you must first evaluate your own health as a leader. While physical health is paramount, the overall health of a leader consists of so much more. The health of a leader can be summarized using the seven main "F's".

Family

There are many definitions for the word family. Merriam-Webster lists eight. Most people will either describe their family as blood relatives (common ancestry), or very close friends. And while the overly used statement, "blood is thicker than water," seems cool to say, for many it's just not true. People who have come from broken, dysfunctional, or abusive homes will find relational safety elsewhere.

BEFORE YOU CAN DEVELOP OTHERS YOU MUST EXAMINE YOUR OWN LEADERSHIP HEALTH.

Whether you consider family to be common ancestry or a clique of your closest friends, to be a healthy person you must foster a healthy family dynamic. Work matters very little when there is instability at home or with personal relationships.

Friends

Just because your family is healthy doesn't mean you don't need friends. Friends can provide a perspective others can't. Ancient Greek tragedian Euripides believed, "One loyal friend is worth ten thousand relatives." Perhaps he just had a bad family dynamic, but his sentiment is able to stand on its own merit.

In fact, the statement we used in the last section, "blood is thicker than water," may not be the full quote. Some modern interpreters have suggested the complete phrase is, "The blood of the covenant is thicker than the water of the womb."

It's often said that the difference between friends and family is choice. You don't get to choose your blood relatives, but the fact that you can select your friends often creates a bond that may not be present in family. Having friends who love when it's hard and speak truth when everyone else is lying may indeed be worth ten thousand relatives.

Future

Where are you going? Sure, you can't predict the future, but you certainly can influence it. Healthy leaders have clear personal and professional goals. We will drift without intention.

Finances

73% of Americans list finances as the #1 stress in life. It's even higher with Gen Z'ers (82%) and millennials (81%).[1] It's terribly hard to focus on anything else when you are over-whelmed by finances. Healthy leaders know how to use money, not be used by money.

Faith

Many people list faith as the reason for their success. Strong faith provides a moral compass when times get hard. Great leaders understand that faith is not a crutch. It's empowering when applied correctly.

Fitness

Money can buy a lot of things. It can buy a vacation, a nice house, and a reliable car. People who have received a terminal diagnosis would give every dime they owned if it meant they'd be healed. When we neglect our physical fitness we neglect the one thing we can't buy. Fitness looks different to everyone, but for our purposes it is a consistent, intentional focus on self-care. Whether you walk every night or become a professional bodybuilder, care for your body so you can live long enough and healthy enough to see your planted seeds grow.

Food

Success, money, and advancement matter very little if you are too sick to enjoy it. While food is something we enjoy, it's also something that keeps us operating at an optimal level. You don't put cheap gas in a Lamborghini so why would you expect to run hard and fast when loaded down with junk?

Make a decision to care for your health and you'll have the opportunity to enjoy the fruits of your harvest.

Top performing leaders understand that to be weak in one area is to feel its effects in other areas of life.

John Maxwell, a leadership expert who has authored more than 70 leadership books, explains this principle as the "Law of the Lid." The Law of the Lid says the success of a team will depend on the lid a leader places on it. Ultimately, it is the leader's responsibility to raise his or her level of personal and professional development. As a result the team will also raise their performance.

For example, a leader with a performance level of a six will never lead a team of 9's and 10's. The team will never rise higher than their leader. A leader with a performance level of six will lead a team that is a five or below.

Leaders want their team to raise output, service, and contributions to the organization, but a leader must raise their lid. If the leader wants a team performing with the competition at an eight level, the leader needs to raise their own leadership level to at least a nine.

Leaders Grow

As Maxwell explains, personal development is a vital component of leadership growth.

To develop others, we must constantly be working on ourselves, but it goes even deeper than this. Leaders should know the answer to the question: Why am I here?

No, not in this physical location reading this text. They must be able to clearly express why they love leading others, or why they desire to lead. Is it because you're looking to make a bigger impact? Do you see it as a way to make more money, or maybe you stepped into leadership reluctantly because your boss asked you to do so.

No matter what brought you into a leadership role, a definitive answer as to why you're here will provide purpose and direction to your team. With clarity, a farmer can bring the highest yield of his/her crops, and with clarity, a leader can live by design with satisfaction. The result will be a bountiful harvest, both personally and professionally.

Understanding your purpose, or knowing your "why," is critical to success.

LEADERSHIP IS MORE ABOUT WHAT YOU ARE BECOMING THAN WHAT YOU ARE DOING.

Clarity is king and it is the farmer's key to a profitable season. Their vision for how an open field can produce a bountiful harvest is unmatched. It's one of many attributes a farmer possesses to bring seed to life.

Leadership clarity propels an organization forward. Before we move forward in this chapter, I want you to define your vision, your purpose, your "why am I here" statement.

I used to think leadership was simply doing a task and helping others do theirs, but I learned leadership is more about who you're becoming than what you're doing.

_____ is here because _____.

(name)   (why you're here)

A good leader understands that without clarity their professional and personal lives will be aimless, frustrating, and depressing. They'll feel defeated more than fulfilled. No matter where you want to be, honest assessment and acceptance of where you are allows you to create change that promotes growth.

As a leader, I had to take uncomfortable personal inventory. In 2016, my highest professional opportunity intersected with my lowest personal moment in life. The best thing I experienced during this tumultuous season was a job promotion. I went from managing 12 team members to overseeing nearly 100 team members.

My life was a roller coaster, but it was the type of ride I orchestrated. It was the type of life I chose. It reeked of uncertainty. My life was a series of sharp turns leading to nowhere and it felt like there was no escape.

I'd drink every day after work until dinner time, pause long enough to eat, and then go back to drinking until bedtime. It was a vicious cycle I lived for nearly two decades and it left me disengaged and drifting from my personal and professional responsibilities.

I remember validating my behavior. "Oh, at least I work," or "At least, I'm taking care of my family." Statements like this are a reflection of a person who refuses to take responsibility and accountability for their actions. Each time I'd say it, I felt better, but deep down I knew something wasn't right.

Like it or not, we're planting seeds every moment of every day and the type of harvest we're producing is a direct reflection of the seeds planted. As much as I tried to justify not being the leader I should have been at work and home, it all caught up to me. My drug and alcohol addiction was severe. Looking back on it, I'm not sure how I kept my job.

Late one summer night in 2015, I found myself rationalizing how much better life would be if I ran from my duties as a husband and father. It was an internal conversation to choose a party life over my family. I made an emotional decision fueled by an intoxicated body and brain.

Overcome by disillusionment, I entered my home and told my wife the worst news any man or woman can hear their spouse say, "I'm leaving." We sat on the bedroom floor and cried. I knew it wasn't what I needed to do, but I wasn't thinking rationally. The choice to leave came from the place of least resistance, and so I ran. I didn't know where I was going or where I'd stay, but I ran anyway.

I walked out of my house and walked away from my wife and two children. I left my daughter, Lexxie (13 years old) and OV (11 years old) to fend for themselves. I made a reckless attempt to satisfy my personal desires, while masking a different persona at work. Like seeds, my choices produced a harvest of weeds and tainted soil where no good thing could flourish.

I had no plan, nowhere to go and lived an aimless life. I spent several nights at a local state park, sleeping in a tent with the exception of the rainy nights that pushed me into my car. I slept in the proverbial bed I made for myself. It sucked, and the restless nights didn't make things any better. All I knew to do was numb the pain with drugs and show up for work every day. I was more concerned with being in attendance than how I showed up for work.

There were tough days, but I refused to change. I refused to plant different seeds.

I was a multi-unit supervisor leading nearly a hundred team members at fourteen sites. This was my largest territory to supervise, and the daily tasks demanded my full attention and energy.

Every day after work, I stopped by a dive bar to drown reality and hope it would send me to sleep peacefully.

In one of my darkest moments as a leader, a father, and a husband, I met an older, kind man — the type of person who helped the house band tote their gear on stage or encourage patrons to tip the bartender extra. He taught me one of the most valuable lessons in an unexpected place.

This wasn't a large space and most patrons there were men stopping by with the same hopes and ambitions. They all wanted to forget about their responsibilities and numb the pain they were running from.

This older man, I assume he had to be around 60 years old, asked, "Why are you here?"

"I like live music and cold beer," I answered, knowing this response wouldn't lead me wrong.

He asked again, "Why are you here?"

The house band played, so I thought his repeated question was an attempt to hear my first answer, so I replied louder and slower so he could read my lips, "I liiike liiiive muuuusic and coooold beeeeeer." His hearing wasn't the issue. I lacked understanding.

Now his face clearly showed my answer wasn't the one he wanted to hear. "I heard you the first time, but I was hoping the second time you'd be honest with me," he sadly replied.

"That's not why you're here," he confirmed. "You're here because you're running from your responsibilities at home and your power to be a great father and husband. Get outta here and go take care of your family and your future."

WHEN WE ARE **UNCLEAR** OF OUR PURPOSE WE LOSE TRACK OF WHO WE ARE SUPPOSED TO **BECOME**.

It was at that moment I realized when we're unclear as to why we're here, we lose track of where we're supposed to be, what we're supposed to do, and who we are supposed to become.

This conversation caused deep reflection in my life. Although I made an uncomfortable bed for myself and family by leaving home, I knew my current situation wasn't where I wanted to be and in order to change my situation, I was first going to need to sow seeds of sacrifice and humility.

This conversation sat heavily on my conscience, like a weighted barbell that you desperately try to push off your chest. I had ignored everything I needed to do, which resulted in feeling down, depressed, and deflated.

Daniel Goleman writes in his bestselling book, Emotional Intelligence, "Exceptional leaders distinguish themselves because of superior self-leadership."

While I thought I was a good leader, I quickly realized the gaps in what I wanted versus who I was. It was then I realized that in order to excel and lead others effectively, I had to first lead myself.

I had to start with my own personal growth and acknowledge the impact my choices were having on my family and at work. It was time to find help for my addiction.

Years prior, my mom mentioned Celebrate Recovery (CR) — a Christ centered, 12 step recovery program for anyone struggling with hurt, pain or addiction of any kind. I googled the organization. Deep down I knew this was my last chance for help and hope. When my Mom mentioned CR in the past, I had no interest. But now I was committed to overcoming this awful, generational battle.

I found an article about a local church hosting a CR group the following week. Too embarrassed to tell my partying friends why I wouldn't be at the bar that night, I snuck away and headed to the group. As I arrived, doubts flooded my mind. I wanted to make a U-turn and leave. Instead, I found the farthest parking spot available and parked.

I sat frozen in the driver's seat. I didn't know who would be in there. I wondered if they'd smell the alcohol on my breath from the beer I had a few hours earlier.

Begrudgingly, I turned the engine off, took the keys out of the ignition and thought, "What do I have to lose?"

I saw some guys shooting basketball outside, and I gravitated in that direction. I hoped by shooting three-pointers, I'd keep enough space between us so my distinct smell wouldn't be detected and allow me time to warm up to this new environment.

As we were shooting hoops, one guy shared with us how he had "used" yesterday but came to the group because he didn't want to keep using.

I wasn't the only one still struggling with addiction. By still struggling I mean, still using hours before the group. As hard as it was to personally recognize this behavior, it comforted me to know that I wasn't alone.

We headed into the building for worship music, a sermon-style message and small group discussions.

I walked out and continued to use the following day.

The following week, I didn't use two days leading up to the group. Now that doesn't sound like much – but for me – it was a milestone accomplishment. My heart, body, and mind began a deeper soul search. It was an inaudible scream for help.

I was supposed to be at home loving my wife and children.
I was supposed to be at home working on becoming a better person.
I was supposed to be doing big things in life.
I was supposed to be a healthy leader.

There were a whole bunch of excuses why I wasn't doing what I was supposed to be doing. I found myself ready to change in the second week of meetings.

The band played a song by Bethel Music called "No Longer Slaves." As they sang the words of the song, one specific verse brought me to tears.

From my mother's womb
You have chosen me.
Love has called my name
I've been born again
Into Your family
Your blood flows through my veins.

I was convicted as I realized my life had purpose the moment it was being created inside my mother's womb. I wasn't fulfilling my purpose, nor was I using my God-given gifts to change the world.

So many people counted on me — my wife, children, brothers, parents, and colleagues. I needed to lead and break free from what held me back from producing profitable results. I pledged my faith to Jesus and made commitments to quit using drugs and alcohol, reconcile my marriage, and become the leader I was designed to be. The band continued to play and repeat the chorus:

I'm no longer a slave to fear.
I am a child of God.
I'm no longer a slave to fear.

I cried like a baby. I finally felt like I could be the leader God created me to be. I called my wife as I left the church and told her about the worship service and the decision I made. She empathetically listened and held on to each word, but I could feel the doubt in her voice. I wasn't discouraged because I knew this was the moment she and many others prayed for. The moment when I would own my potential and begin to create a better life.

I'd been away from my family for eight months. This was a shallow attempt to reconcile all that had been lost. It was going to take time, but I took the first step.

No matter how well things were going at work, I needed to overcome adversity and win at home. The road to reconciliation with my wife and children proved long and hard, but it forever shaped future generations.

In the summer of 2016, I returned home committed to living a sober life and to restoring our family bond. I'm grateful to my wife, Damaris and children, who encouraged me to heal and be the man they knew I could be.

Everyone has some type of vice. Some of you have only one, while others of us have too many to count. It could be anger, lack of confidence, smoking, not being coachable, drugs, lack of focus, control, micromanaging, or more.

It requires an honest evaluation of where you currently are and a commitment to being the best you can be at work and at home in order to produce the highest yield.

Your organization, your life, your family, and your legacy need the best you, the best possible version of yourself. This version will determine what you produce at work and in life.

What good is a man or woman if they're leading others at work but not leading themselves and their families?

You've probably heard the saying, "Leave your personal life at home, don't bring it to work."

This is the furthest thing from the truth. Everywhere we go, there we are — every part of us, including the good, bad and the ugly.

My personal life spilled into my professional life. My promotion in 2016 and personal struggles erupted into a perfect storm which catapulted me into responsibilities I'd never experienced before. It was perfect timing, but I had decisions to make. Either lose it all — new career, family, and future — or take the steps to address my struggles.

I chose to own my failures and weaknesses and began a deep track of personal, spiritual, and professional development. There was no one to blame but me. It was time to step up and form my legacy.

A leader is responsible for his or her proverbial farm. Their duty is to cultivate the open space and create the highest yield possible.

With every new opportunity, every new seed I planted, and every weed I pulled, I had to answer the question, Why am I here? The clearer I am on this statement, the better I can work on what needs to be accomplished in my calling as a leader at work, home and in the community.

My answer evolves at times, but it's rooted in a few things that will never disappear — my family, faith, leadership, and legacy.

John Maxwell gave one of the best quotes on success when he said, "I define success when the people who know me the best love and respect the most."

I hope others will be able to say:

Joe guided his children and family towards a deeper love with Jesus and with all people around the world. They did this by reflecting Him in their thoughts, actions, and words.

Joe was the founder of New Leaf Leadership - a consulting and leadership development company — where he taught leaders how to reap the highest yield in their organizations and in their personal lives by unlocking their inner farmer to pull the weeds, prepare the soil, plant the seeds, and produce results at work and in life.

Joe developed New Leaf Farm to equip people and organizations to "turn a new leaf" and write new chapters in their business and life. NLF is the premier leadership retreat space connecting leaders from around the world where they cultivate leadership skills in the classroom while improving social and emotional wellness outside with their hands in the garden dirt.

While your description of the *ideal you* may vary, it's important to note there are no right or wrong answers. It's yours. Take your time and fill in the blanks one more time below.

_____ is here because _____.
    (name)   (why you're here)

Sustainable Leadership vs. Conventional Leadership

"If you always do things the way you've always done, you'll always get what you've always had." - Jessie Potter

Conventional leadership practices are becoming increasingly ineffective. The old way of leading others is typically expressed in a form of top-down leadership. Thoughts like, *they should do as I say because I'm the boss*, may be pervasive in work cultures but that doesn't mean they are healthy environments. Insecure, absolute statements such as this often mask a leader's insecurities. They believe it's better to be a dictator than a victim. Both are destructive to team dynamics and the future of an organization.

Another conventional approach is to place more focus on productivity and less on people. Profit over people may impress shareholders but it will undermine the organization's sustainability.

Neither method, power or profit over people, will sustain long-term results without harmful effects to the soil (culture) and seed (people). It may produce a high yield in the form of dollars, but like a blossoming peach orchard with no workers, the harvest will not reap rewards if teams are divided or absent.

In contrast, sustainable leadership practices focus on profit, yes, but not at the expense of its people.

Sustainable leadership practices are taking organizations by storm and lead them to higher profits, increased productivity, and improved job satisfaction due to focused efforts on culture and purpose.

It's similar to different farming methods: sustainable and conventional.

According to USDA.gov, sustainable farming practices "are intended to protect the environment, expand the Earth's natural resource base, and maintain and improve soil fertility."[2] It seeks to:

- Increase profitable farm income.
- Promote environmental stewardship.
- Enhance quality of life for farm families and communities.
- Increase production for human food and fiber needs.

As more farmers become conscious of the environmental impact, sustainable agriculture is growing in popularity and adoption. Widespread adoption is happening due in part to sustainable farming's effectiveness to increase productivity with less space, more research on environmentally sound practices and a more holistic approach to allow nature to run its course.

While sustainable farming practices make sense, sustainable leadership is an approach that focuses on larger impact leaders play at work. Dr Jenny Davidson, Executive MBA Degree Program Director at Newcastle University Business School, describes sustainable leadership as "all about adopting a responsible approach to the way that we lead, stopping to think about the wider impact of our actions on society and the environment. This might mean considering our wider stakeholder group, the natural systems within which we are operating and their limits."[3]

Where conventional leadership leans towards a mentality of do more and give more at all costs, sustainable leadership places a team member's overall health — emotional, mental, physical, spiritual and financial — as high-ranking priority.

Sustainable leaders recognize the interconnectivity between people, procedures, output and profits and address points of tension to avoid burnout or poor performance. They know quality in each area, not one facet alone, gives their organization the best chance to compete long term.

Like a sustainable farmer, a sustainable leader takes all things into account when planning for success. They never sacrifice their goal to produce the highest quality of the highest yield but instead, they increase the quality of their people, environment and create a better future for themselves, their families and their communities.

Characteristics such as diligence, resourcefulness, flexibility, observance, and the ability to practice self-care are valuable attributes sustainable farmers possess. But above all, a farmer's secret tools are patience and a deep belief in their seed. They believe it will produce a harvest.

Patience is necessary because a farmer's reward comes slow. A corn farmer may wait four to six months before seeing a harvest, while an asparagus farmer won't see full production until year three and beyond.

Practicing patience is essential when leading. Leaders want innovative ideas to come to fruition immediately, but they must delay gratification and diligently wait. Waiting isn't just giving people or projects time. It's also how you wait. Patience in the workplace is important but doing it without complaining or rushing the process just to meet deadlines shows high emotional intelligence.

I once worked for a leader who didn't practice patience. He always seemed too busy completing the next task and continuously lost sight of the most important thing, his people. His number one focus was his way, right now, without any input from others. His authoritarian leadership style created a tense atmosphere and caused anxiety and separation. In high stress times, he would lose his temper and verbally attack team members. His laser focus on quick results led to isolation and poor team morale. He lacked the patience needed to allow others to assist, even if it wasn't at his preferred speed.

Leadership and patience work hand-in-hand, as we give our team the space, time and belief, they will bloom. As we show confidence in their abilities and help develop their skill, they are empowered to follow through on tasks. It will take time and a deep level of empathy for others as we politely and patiently wait for the harvest to arrive. What do you do in the meantime? You must believe something is happening even when you can't see it.

We live in a world that longs for instant gratification. This leads us to believe we are failing if we don't experience immediate results. Gary Vaynerchuk, Chairman of VaynerX, CEO of VaynerMedia, 5-Time NYT Bestselling Author says, "Play the long game." The long game is the ability to put in the work today for success three, five or seven years down the road. It's putting in the work early and often and expecting the biggest payoff to come later. Yes, you'll learn lessons and make some short term gains, but the highest yields come through persevering with positivity and believing as you wait.

A leader loves the process, trusts the process, and believes in the process with an unwavering commitment. They know the harvest is coming so they wait patiently, but confidently for the payoff.

HARVEST IMPLEMENTATION EXERCISE
Farmer Readiness

PURPOSE: Embody your, "Why I'm here?" statement.

_____ is here because _____.
  (name)   (why you're here)

Commit to reading this statement every morning.

Do this before checking email, scrolling through social media and before brushing your teeth. Nah, scratch that. Write it on the mirror and see it while you're brushing your teeth and with a fresh, clean mouth boldly declare it for the entire house to hear.

See your organization as a sustainable farm, ready to grow by caring for your people, the environment and the community you live in.

Let 'em know the harvest is coming!

CHAPTER 5
The Seasons

To everything there is a season,
> and a time for every purpose under heaven:
a time to be born and a time to die,
> a time to plant and a time to uproot,
a time to kill and a time to heal,
> a time to break down and a time to build,
a time to weep and a time to laugh,
> a time to mourn and a time to dance,
a time to cast away stones and a time to gather stones together,
> a time to embrace and a time to refrain from embracing,
a time to search and a time to count as lost,
> a time to keep and a time to discard,
a time to tear and a time to mend,
> a time to be silent and a time to speak,
a time to love and a time to hate,
> a time for war and a time for peace.

- Ecclesiastes 3:1-8

S o many quality ideas, projects, and people have been tossed by the wayside and forgotten like an old copper penny on the side of the road.

A farmer leads with a keen understanding that everything has a season and maybe, just maybe, it's not the fault of the seed, the soil or the farmer. Timing is everything.

In my earlier years of gardening, I wanted to grow zucchini. I knew the seed was good because it came from the same seed packet that produced a harvest earlier in the season. The soil was perfectly conditioned for a healthy harvest as well. Although I was newer to gardening, I had an ability to cultivate, nurture, and harvest multiple varieties of vegetables including zucchini. My past success gave me the confidence to do it all over again. All three components were there — good seed, good soil and a knowledgeable farmer.

It's easy to use past success as an indicator for future success without considering the external conditions may have changed. Don't rest on yesterday's success without taking into consideration that today isn't yesterday and tomorrow may require a new approach.

Past success blinded me. All I could think about was my wife's zucchini bread. If I could only grow more, we could have a surplus of her freshly baked bread.

I shoveled, piercing through the black gold until the South Carolina red clay revealed itself. Mixing the two soils together, I placed the seed on top of the ready soil mixture.

With everything in place, I sprinkled enough water to moisten the soil and went in for the night. Each day, I checked for weeds and added water when needed. Two weeks passed until the first green sprout sprang up from the black soil.

My confidence grew as signs of growth looked much like the earlier harvest. After weeks of checking on the plants, it never produced a single vegetable. It produced healthy leaves and a healthy-looking plant but not a single vegetable.

Puzzled, I continued to nurture it, hoping my actions would encourage the first squash blossom.

Nothing changed.

Perplexed by the plant's inability to produce, I finally asked my gardening mentor what I was doing wrong.

He said, "You're not seeing results because it's the wrong season."

I was puzzled because everything seemed to be in similar conditions earlier when it was produced. Daytime air temperatures felt like the earlier summer months, but night temperatures dropped drastically and lowered the soil temperature. Thus, the soil couldn't sustain temperatures needed to produce what this warm soil loving plant needed.

Organizational success is similar. What worked once may not produce the same results in a different season. Conversely, what didn't work before may work today. Successful leaders understand timing and how to prepare and launch at just the right time. They know how to exercise proper business kairos.

Kairos is a Greek word meaning, "A time when conditions are right for the accomplishment of a crucial action: the opportune and decisive moment."

Kairos is one of two Greek words meaning time. The other, kronos, means clock time or chronological time whereas kairos specifically address timed precision. In ancient Greek times, Kairos is said to describe archery and weaving. In archery, kairos defines the precise moment when an archer must release the arrow to pierce an intended target. In weaving, kairos denotes the moment in which an instrument weaves into the threads of a loom.[1]

A leader's ability to precisely interpret the room, the climate and the market to make decisions is a leader's sixth sense. When decisions are made at the right time, it can be seen as pure genius. Timing is everything. Submitting a resumé a day late may cost you the job of your dreams. Leaving your house at the wrong time may cause you to experience overwhelming traffic. If you invested heavily in Tesla stock in 2011 you may be a millionaire today. Investing in Tesla now will be more difficult.

Timing is everything. I may not be much of a baker, but I know when a cake is left in the oven too long it will be dry, not moist. I know most chefs prefer their steaks cooked medium rare.

Taking the steak off at just the right time is crucial. Timing is everything. The difference between a strike out and a home run is timing. Good timing is critical to success, but how can you tell if your timing is good? When it comes to your leadership career, you want to strike while the iron's hot, but you also want to avoid taking on so much that you become overextended. You may even behave unprofessionally by getting behind on deadlines, communicating poorly, or even losing your job.

When you focus on strategic timing you can make sure everything happens at the right time when it should, without having to rush through any part of it. Strategic timing may look different to different people, but the concepts are fundamentally the same. We all get the same 168 hours each week and what we do with those hours determines the direction of our business, our quality of life, and our measure of fulfillment.

I want to be incredibly practical in this chapter so let's discuss some good time management systems that will benefit your personal and professional life.

Time Tracking

Time and money can often approach with similar efficiencies. For instance, a budget tells your money where it's going to go instead of wondering where it went. A schedule tells your time where it is going to go instead of wondering where it went.

Some people are averse to keeping a detailed, structured schedule, but I believe it's because they misunderstand the benefits. A schedule does not limit your freedom, it gives you more. If you do not hold a strong conviction as to where your time should go, people will craft your schedule for you, but it will be for their benefit and not yours.

If you are not clear on your purpose, short-term and long-term goals, and where your time should go for optimal impact, you will thrive only in your ineffectiveness. Time can be spent or invested. It can be wasted or yield a high ROI; it all depends on what you do with it. The average adult watches 3 hours of television a day.[2] That's 21 hours in a week, so did you really not have time to complete that project? Or did you spend 15% of your week staring at a tv screen?

One proven way to evaluate your time usage is to craft a planned-versus-actual schedule. You can use an excel spreadsheet or traditional calendar, but the goal is to get an accurate assessment of how you use your time. Here's how it works:

Step 1:

Log every minute of every day for an entire week. You can break it down into increments of 15 minutes. For instance, if you worked from 7am to 1pm, you can simply write "work" during that time on your calendar. You don't need to list every single minute you spent at work. If you spent 8 hours that week, write it down.

If you spent 5 hours on social media, write it down. Include hygiene, mourning routines, bedtime routines, commute time, and sleep.

At the end of your week the totality of your activity should equal 168 hours. This may seem tedious, but it's not as hard as you think. Large portions of your life are repetitive. They are called anchor times. Anchor times are consistent times you can build a schedule around. Some examples of anchor times are the time you leave for work, the time you eat meals, work hours, and bedtime.

Step 2:

Make a list of what you'd like to accomplish the following week. You can list the to-do's however you'd like, but I'd suggest listing the high-priority items first, followed by the lower priority items. High priority items are not just work related. It could be organizing your closet or cleaning the gutters. They are simply projects that must get done and chances are you've procrastinated completing them. You may need a separate list for work and home.

Next, determine how long it will take you to complete those items. Will it take 30 minutes to clean and organize the closet? An hour? Two hours? Mark the estimated time on the list next to the item.

Now you're going to put the list onto your calendar. Start by filling in your anchor times, followed by the high priority to-do's. This is what you plan to do. I understand, plans can change. That's life. Your schedule is not written in stone, it's a living organism that ebbs and flows with the difficulties and opportunities of life. But by planning your schedule in advance you'll be better equipped to maneuver those difficulties.

Step 3:

Here comes the kicker - accountability. Sit down with your spouse, oversight, or a close friend and ask them to hold you accountable to your planned calendar. Write down what you actually did next to what you had planned to do. What went right?

What went wrong? Did you underestimate the time it would take to complete a project?

Now, rinse and repeat. If you do this every week and invite someone to hold you accountable to your goals, you'll find you can accomplish more than you ever thought possible.

White Space

Effective leaders use their calendars as a guardrail. Scheduling white space means blocking off several hours for thinking, creativity, and problem solving. While you may not be working on a tangible goal, you are proactively creating a space where you can focus on a bigger picture.

When an employee, co-worker, or client asks to meet during this time you can kindly decline. You don't have to give details, just reply, "I'm sorry, I'm unavailable during that time. Let's look at another day / time that may work."

Pomodoro Technique

Do you have trouble focusing? You may need some additional structure that allows for shorter bursts of work coupled with a little wandering. Welcome to the Pomodoro Technique. Developed in the 1980s, this technique has six key steps:[3]

1. Decide on the task
2. Set a timer for 25 minutes
3. Work on the task
4. End work when the timer expires. Take a 5–10 minute break.
5. Repeat three more times.
6. After the fourth "pomodoro," take a 20-30 minute break.

Those who benefit the most from the pomodoro technique are those who:[4]

- Find little distractions often derail the whole workday
- Consistently work past the point of optimal productivity
- Have lots of open-ended work that could take unlimited amounts of time (e.g., studying for an exam, research for a blog post, etc.)
- Are overly optimistic when it comes to how much you can get done in a day
- Enjoy gamified goal setting

No matter the technique, timing is everything. By functioning efficiently you'll not miss key seasons.

Leaders who properly practice kairos are seen as opportunistic and know how to take advantage of opportunities. While many leaders are looking for the next big idea to implement or seed to plant, success comes from understanding that there is work to be done in every season.

Along with understanding the right time for an activity, it's also vital to know when to pull back and pause. Not every season is the right time for the next big thing. Preparation in each season is important to ensure success for the "big" moment.

Every season isn't a time for planting. As the '70s band "The Byrds" so beautifully illustrated,

> *To everything (turn, turn, turn),*
> *There is a season (turn, turn, turn),*
> *And a time to every purpose, under heaven.*

Local farmer Katie Donohoe demonstrated this point one February afternoon when I stopped by to assist with winter farm chores. The grapevines were dry and the excess limbs weighed down the steel cables tied to the T-posts. Katie explained why cutting away the extra growth, or pruning, was necessary to optimize a healthier, higher yield in the summer.

Grapevines can produce fruit without pruning but doing it annually enables the grapevine to produce at its full growth potential. She pointed out that while the grapevines aren't produced in winter, the preparation work — pulling the weeds and pruning — is as important as the actual growing and harvesting seasons.

Farmers use the winter months to prepare for planting and harvest seasons. They optimize the down time by taking proactive steps to set up their farm for success. During the winter months, you may also find farmers maintaining equipment, pruning vines and trees and planting cover crops to protect and enhance the soil.

Each step taken is a proactive one because when temperatures warm and planting season approaches, there is no time to do what should've been done during the slower growth season.

While harvest time is a leader's favorite time, there is work to be done in every season to prepare for the highest yielding harvest. An organization's season, like winter, is a time to be proactive. The fields are empty but the opportunities to prepare are overflowing.

An Organization's Life Cycle

There are four general stages to a company; Dream, Develop, Defend, and Death. Every organization begins with a dream. That dream may appear in various forms, from a technological breakthrough to a new way of managing customers. Whether the dream was to create the best pancake or build a statue, the dream provided the direction, passion, and discipline needed to see it come to fruition.

Eventually the dream had to become a reality. You don't make money from dreams. You make money from developing those dreams into a tangible product or service. It takes sweat, time, emotion, failure, and fatigue to see a dream take shape. After long days, strenuous weeks, and countless years you will see the fruit of your labor. The dream has become a reality. You have developed it into something beautiful. Then the unexpected happens. You stop dreaming.

Once you stop dreaming and the developing stage has run its course, an organization often settles into the "defend" stage. During this stage the company tries to replicate what brought it this far and if challenged, they'll defend themselves by looking at past accomplishments. This is disheartening and often leads to lower company morale, higher turnover of top talent, and a general air of malaise.

When a company sits in defense for too long, death is not far behind. The products are no longer innovative, the competition has caught up or surpassed them, or the old regime transitions with no fresh vision for the future.

For a company to be continually viable they must live in the dream and develop stages, jumping repeatedly from one to the next.

The same goes for a leader. You are not the same person you were ten years ago. You are either dreaming and developing or you are defending and dying. There is no easy way around it. A great leader constantly evaluates their life, work, and family to see how they can move forward in unity. If you begin to defend your past actions instead of inviting new, unusual, or in some cases overwhelming ideas, you'll lose your relative value and find yourself straddling the fence of insignificance.

Procrastination is not an excuse. It can be easy to wait for just the right time and conditions. Rarely, if ever, do you have perfect conditions to start. Each leader must take advantage of each season to progress successfully to the next season.

Organizations can also use the down time to prepare for busier months. Leaders who take advantage of the winter months of business can produce higher yields and set the organization up for sustained success.

While some would argue there is no luck found in four-leaf clovers or horseshoes, there are ample chances for "luck" when there is preparation. Seneca, the famous Roman stoic once said, "Luck is when preparation meets opportunity."

When preparation happens in the slower times, leaders position their teams for opportune times. While the competition finds themselves getting ready once the opportunity arises, proactive leaders are in position and ready to act. Each organization has unique slow and busy seasons. The question is, do you know what season you are in? Leaders who don't schedule white space, manage expectations, or set aside time to dream will often lack the discernment needed to identify and navigate the seasons.

"We never have enough time" is a cry of those in the trenches, but the numbers can provide a better analysis of less productive times. Some focus areas during slow seasons could include:

- Cross-training team members,
- Maintaining equipment,
- Focusing on mental health and overall team wellness,
- Updating software,
- Initiating plans for new projects, or evaluating current systems.

Each task may not produce the moment, but it creates space for higher, healthier growth. Leaders who take time to maximize slower months will improve their ability to handle the busier seasons.

When you maximize each season you will experience better results at work and in life.

- *Every season can't be a planting season.*
- *Every season can't be a harvest season.*
- *Every season does present an opportunity to grow, even if it's through preparation alone.*

What are you doing to optimize each season?

Author's Note:

This book was written during my business's winter months. There was a gap when I wouldn't be on the road speaking as much during a two-month period. Writing a book was identified as a much needed activity during the busy season but, at that time, I didn't

WHEN YOU MAXIMIZE EACH SEASON YOU WILL EXPERIENCE BETTER RESULTS AT WORK AND IN LIFE.

have space to write it. It's one of two activities that were identified as much needed for the business. It was all about timing because I needed the book written before in-person speaking engagements increased in order to promote and sell copies. Kairos is essential for successful new product launches and for optimizing results from current project enhancements.

HARVEST IMPLEMENTATION EXERCISE
The Seasons

Identify the slow seasons. These are the slowest times when business isn't producing at annual peak levels. It could be once a year or there may be multiple seasons. It could be one day or it could be one month.

After identifying the slow season, establish a list of 2-3 activities that typically are placed lower on the priority list. The goal here is to use each activity to make the slower times more productive, more efficient and more sustainable.

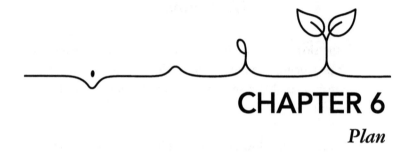

CHAPTER 6
Plan

"If you aim at nothing, you will hit every time." - Zig Ziglar

The Seeds to Success framework explained over the next four chapters has many functions. It applies to personal results, professional projects, fitness, finance, or any other area you'd like to produce gains. The most important part is to know that there are no limitations on implementation.

This was a system I used to overcome a 16-year battle with drugs and alcohol, launch a six-figure leadership development company, and start a nonprofit, A New Leaf Farm, dedicated to helping migrant families "turn a new leaf" while also serving as a leadership retreat helping organizations write new chapters for their businesses.

It's an easy-to-apply method that helps structure ideas and identify each step needed to produce a healthy yield.

To demonstrate how the Seeds to Success framework produces better results in life and work, I chose two areas where people commonly struggle. Those areas are personal fitness and communication at work.

I trust you'll find immense value as we talk about how to go from idea (seed) to producing results (success). Ready to learn? Let's go!

Polaris

The North Star, also known as Polaris, is approximately 433 light-years away from the earth. It's not the brightest star in the sky but it's widely known by astronomers and navigators alike. Why? Because of its position. It is located directly above the earth's north pole. If ever you are disoriented or lost, simply locate the North Pole and you'll be able to find your way home.

Many people have a north star in business and at home. It is the guiding principle that keeps them grounded, focused, and moving steadily in the right direction. Those who do not have a proverbial north star find themselves treading water, never able to get ahead. Why? Well, you can't get ahead if you don't know where you're going to begin with.

Do you have a north star in your business? At home? Knowing where you're heading provides clarity, guides spontaneity, and sparks the most dedicated procrastinator. Plans are not meant to be unbreakable laws, but rather to serve as a guide. Plans guide you when you're frustrated, perplexed, or just experiencing a bad season.

Pause and take a moment to reflect. Do you have a north star in your business? How about in your personal life? It's crucial to establish a clear sense of direction, for knowing where you're heading brings about clarity, guides your actions in moments of spontaneity, and even ignites the motivation of the most dedicated procrastinator. Remember, plans are not rigid and unbreakable laws; rather, they serve as reliable guides, especially during times of frustration, confusion, or when life throws challenges your way.

Before you continue on this journey, I implore you to pause and make a deliberate decision. Take a step back and identify one thing, although you don't have to limit yourself to just one. Start with clarity, as your answer will provide you with a definitive direction. Not only will it guide you, but it will also influence those around you. The more focused your gaze, the clearer your vision becomes, leading you more swiftly toward your desired destination. As a result, you'll witness the emergence of tangible outcomes, the amplification of your impact, and an increased attraction towards your mission.

Allow me to share my personal experience with you. It all began with a fundamental question: "Why am I here on earth?" Answering this question laid the foundation for my next inquiry: "What do I want to produce?" By taking the time to reflect on these profound inquiries, I set myself on a path guided by purpose, ensuring that every step I took aligned with my true aspirations.

Your answer will change as you move forward because each new season brings a new level of desired results. Think of this process from a farmer's perspective. The farmer doesn't focus their thoughts on the Farmer's Almanac, their competitors, or last year's performance. Their top focus is on what crop they want to produce and how much they want to yield this season.

A farmer knows specifically what they want to produce and they begin by mapping a plan. It isn't a coincidence that the farmer sells his harvest in the produce section of a grocery store. When you think about what you want to produce, think about what you are taking to the market. What are you exchanging for consumer goods or money?

The farmer asks, "Will I need to produce 1,000 pounds of Roma tomatoes, 100 bushels of corn or 500 bunches of cilantro?" They decide what's needed first for their family and business and then work backwards from there.

Stephen Covey, author of The 7 Habits of Highly Effective People, explained it as "starting with the end in mind." What is the end you have in mind? That is your Polaris, your north star. Set your sights on the goal and de-construct the process until you arrive at where you are right now.

WHAT GOT YOU HERE WILL NOT BE **ENOUGH** TO GET YOU THERE. YOU NEED A **PLAN**.

Arriving at that goal will not be easy. You do not currently have the skillset to get there. That is why a personal growth plan is important. You will have to change, adapt, and develop into the person who can take your family or business to the next level. What got you here will not be enough to get you there. You'll need a plan.

Personal Growth Plan

I used this same approach when I became a school nutrition administrator. I wanted to produce results in my personal health as well as develop a leadership training program at work.

I started with my personal growth because I knew to be a better leader, I had to be the best version of myself. While I needed to improve in many areas, I focused on becoming physi-cally healthier.

The perfect time to define the direction of my fitness jour-ney was in 2017 when my wife was pregnant with our third child, Isabella. We were both in our mid-thirties and I felt the urgency to produce a healthier lifestyle. Having a healthy body would yield high dividends in the present and future. I want to be the seventy year old grandfather who has enough energy and stamina to run around with my grandchildren without physical limitations. I want to set a standard for future generations.

If you are already in great shape, this may not be a big, lofty goal. If you are terribly out of shape this may be the toughest thing you've ever done, but the payoff will be worth the effort. In his book, Built to Last, Jim Collins calls this a "big, hairy, audacious goal", or BHAG.[1]

A BHAG is a clear and compelling goal for your organization or family to strive for. It is not an unachievable pipe dream. That would be an act of cruelty for an organization who is looking for its footing, its direction, its Polaris. No, a BHAG is a goal that energizes your team. It gives them something to strive for.

When I had a clear picture of what I wanted to produce, I was able to form a clear and decisive action plan. The end goal aids the process of achievement and reduces the time needed to attain the desired outcome.

Plans are not restraints. They are freedom. Dale Carnegie observed, "An hour of planning can save you 10 hours of doing." Strategizing your steps will save you time and money. Planning before doing improves what you do, how you do it, and when you do it.

You'll find the word plan before plant in the dictionary because order is essential to producing the life and business of your dreams. Planning prioritizes proactive management versus reactive management. There are three crucial steps to designing a formidable plan.

1.   Visualization
2.   Written goals
3.   Counting the costs

Visualization

Can you see, feel, hear, taste and touch what it would be like to achieve your end goal?

Visualization, according to the American Psychological Association (APA), is "the process of creating a visual image in one's mind or mentally rehearsing a planned movement in order to learn skills or enhance performance."

Visualization is an exercise of mentally envisioning what you want to happen or feel before making it a reality. It is a well-documented exercise many top performing athletes use to cultivate a competitive advantage and to build emotional wellness and rejuvenation.

Michael Jordan, the six-time NBA champion and arguably the greatest professional basketball player of all time, said this about visualization, "Every time I feel tired while exercising and training, I close my eyes to see that picture, to see that list with my name. This usually motivates me to work again."

Jordan used visualization to see his end goal and used it as an intrinsic motivation tool to keep pushing during challenging times, refusing to surrender to pain and discomfort.

Practicing visualization before taking action improves clarity and assists a holistic approach to producing results. Visualization is similar to forms of meditation. It requires a quiet place where you can sit, close your eyes, and think without any distractions. As "froo froo" as it sounds, it's often why the world's best athletes consistently make clutch plays on the biggest stages.

Everyone's end game is different. You can't copy/paste success, but you can mimic the principles proven by successful people and organizations. As I visualize my own personal success, I can't help but think about a similar turning point for John Maxwell. He writes,

> Instead of acclaim or advancement or achievement, I decided that for me, Success means having those closest to me love and respect me the most. This made success for me possible only if I included my wife and children in the journey. From that

moment on, my success depended on putting my family first. If you want to truly succeed in this life, you need to ask yourself a question: Is your pursuit of success drawing you closer to — or farther from — the most important people in your life?[2]

This perspective had a profound impact on me and forever shaped my definition of success. Now, when I visualize what I would look like as a successful speaker, entrepreneur, or business owner, I think of my family and those around me.

Allow me to give you a peek into my world. When I think of success, here is what comes to mind.

My wife seated on our enclosed sun porch overlooking the pool and backyard. The sounds of birds perched in the mature yellow apple trees penetrate the room's silence.

The scents of a morning breakfast float ahead of my steps as I bring two plates filled with scrambled egg whites with caramelized onions, spinach, and broccoli with a side of buttered, halved wheat toast finished with house-made fig preserves.

The morning sun ricochets off the vibrant colors inside two pint-sized Mason jars filled with freshly squeezed orange juice. A separate liter-sized carafe and two filled Collins glasses sweat on the table as the cold water waits to quench morning hydration.

As we slowly eat and chat about the fun-filled moments from the night before, we hear the sounds of laughter and tiny steps coming our way. There they are, our grandchildren, walking towards us with sleepy eyes, messy hair and pajamas dragging the floor. I pick them up and sit them on my lap to cherish their warm embrace.

After a few minutes, we make our way towards the kitchen island to see what they're having for breakfast. I have to convince them that chocolate cupcakes aren't on the breakfast menu. We decide on pancakes.

Our grandchildren are standing in the wooden dining table chair as they begin mixing batter and spooning each pancake into the pan. As they're mixing, I open the kitchen curtains to see how many people are already on the beach.

Excitement builds as the crowds begin to form and we begin talking about the waves we'll ride.

"Grandpa, we love your house," my grandson says with a grin. Smiling, I nod and reply, "It's almost too good to be true, huh?" Little does he know, I had visualized this moment decades earlier.

After breakfast, we head outside and look at the shells picked during the previous night's sunset walk on the beach and laugh about how we're going to do it all over again today.

We pack the coolers, tents, and sand toys and head to the beach. As we pass by our favorite spots, they ask, "Grandpa, can we please have a limber after lunch?"

Without hesitation, I answer, "Absolutely." Never once considering the expense or the fact they're asking about dessert-like treats before lunch.

A cunning smile overtakes my face as joy and peace flood my body. Recognizing this is my Michael Jordan moment, I'm invigorated with life and energy all over again.

I watch our grandchildren run towards the approaching waves as I set up the tents. I take off my shirt and sandals and rush to join them. I pick up my grandson to save him from the crashing waves. He's overjoyed with laughter as I hoist him high in the air as the two of us twirl into the ocean. As we splash in the Atlantic Ocean waves, I exhale deeply and slowly, realizing this is why planning, visualizing, and taking action is so important.

Jack Nicklaus, one of the greatest golfers of all time, said, "I never hit a shot, not even in practice, without having a very sharp in-focus picture of it in my head."

From the inception of this plan, my routine is to wake up every morning, envision the scene, and believe it will happen. You must persistently see and believe. I think about this moment when I wake up in the morning, when I am tempted to skip my workout, and when I decline the thoughts of drug and alcohol use. I think about it again when I lay my head down on the pillow at night.

Visualization is not hocus-pocus witchcraft. It's a system, a deep belief, and a way to plan what you want to produce. But it doesn't stop there, because visualization alone is just a dream. A wish. Visualization is just the beginning.

Once you know what you want to produce and have a clear picture of what it looks and feels like, the next step is to go from mental (visualization) to physical. That's right, you must be willing to put in the work to achieve what you've visualized. It is not someone else's responsibility to fulfill your dream. Success is not built on a foundation of excuses.

Vernon Brundage bluntly stated, "Excuses are monuments of nothingness. They build bridges to nowhere. Those of us who use these tools of incompetence seldom become anything but nothing at all."

S.M.A.T. Goals and Counting the Costs

A written plan consist of two components: costs and goals. Let's tackle the cost piece first. While many may consider the financial cost of a project or commitment, they often fail to comprehend the supplementary resources needed to reach the goal, including but not limited to time, energy, and people. You will understand the total investment when you take all aspects into consideration.

I regularly meet leaders who are excited to embark on a new leadership journey. They order business cards, shop for a new laptop and bag and set off on their career journey. They're enamored with what leadership looks like but not what it will cost. They can be more interested in purchasing the latest equipment and stylish bag than developing a comprehensive plan for their business or venture.

Once enlightened to the vast amount of preparation and work needed to establish and execute the plan to reach their visualized goal, they may battle feelings of inadequacy, failure, or fear. Dejected, they may utter, "I didn't realize there was so much to it." They begin with zeal but quickly flame out because they never calculated the costs associated with producing results.

Sacrifices must be made in order to achieve success. Counting the costs isn't an exact science, but it's important to consider every measurable cost and write it down.

The cost piece will change over time but your willingness to consistently pay the price should be fixed. If you're unwilling to acknowledge the costs or are not committed to pay them, you'll never yield the harvest you desire.

Visionary leaders are unique in that they see the cost but are not discouraged by it. Knowing the costs should only prepare you, never stop you.

John Maxwell often shares a story of an encounter he had while signing books following a speaking engagement. A young man approached him and said, "I've got it. I know what I want to do with my life. I want to do what you do." John Maxwell responded, "If you want to do what I do, you have to be willing to did what I did." Yes, you read that right.

That statement may not be grammatically correct, but it is operationally accurate. Maxwell was willing to pay the price in his small, day to day choices and the result compounded exponentially over time.

James Clear, author of the best-selling book Atomic Habits: An Easy and Proven Way to Build Good Habits and Break Bad Ones, adds, "All big things come from small beginnings. The seed of every habit is a single, tiny decision. But as that decision is repeated, a habit sprouts and grows stronger. Roots entrench themselves and branches grow. The task of breaking a bad habit is like uprooting a powerful oak within us. And the task of building a good habit is like cultivating a delicate flower one day at a time."[3]

Counting costs provides realistic metrics of what sacrifices and commitment are involved to achieve your success. From personal experience, I counted the costs up front because I knew what would be required long before I started down the path. I had a multi-generational mindset and it would require a healthy dose of fortitude mixed with stretch goals and high expectations. To produce a healthy mind, body, and financial security for my grandchildren, I knew I had to count the cost from the beginning. With preparation comes an increased chance of success.

As you calculate the cost, it's important to write it down. It may not be perfect in its genesis, but progress is progress, no matter how slow it may be. When I decided to count the cost, here is what I wrote down:

Money - $25 for a monthly gym membership, $40 for two pairs of gym shorts, $80 for shoes, $100 increase in grocery budget for healthier choices.

Time - waking up at 3:45 a.m. to workout before work.
Entertainment - I would miss several shows due to an earlier bedtime but was willing to do what needed to be done over what felt the best at the time.

Meals - mean an inability to eat everything I wanted. Living in the South makes this harder because saying no to kale chips is easy but denying fried chicken breast, banana pudding and sweet tea feels sacrilegious.

People - Everyone won't follow you on your new journey. I found people share time with those with whom they share common interests. I stopped going to parties, bars and discontinued the late-night binges and as a result, I lost friends and acquaintances. The more I focused on becoming healthier, the more my circle of friends changed. I found myself surrounded by people who also wanted to better themselves.

Proverbs 27:17 says, "As iron sharpens iron, so one man sharpens another." I never found this to be more true than when I found my north star and refused to deviate from it.

Calculating the needed investments early aids your ability to stick with your plan. If you know what resources are available and what structures must be formed during the planning process you'll be equipped to receive the harvest when it comes. Many know how to produce a goal but then don't understand how to maximize their yield once it arrives.

My plan will continue to change over the years, and so will the costs, but my commitment to making a way despite the costs won't change. Stay committed to the end goal, even it means you are forced to take the occasional detour to get there.

The goal behind counting the costs is to set your mind up for success. If you verbally agree to what the costs might be, your chances of paying the costs will increase when they come due. There is no need to waste time or effort if you're going to give up when it comes time to pay the bill.

I'm using this goal as an example of a long-term harvest, but the planning works for a short-term goal as well.

This is evident when one considers planting a fruit orchard versus a tomato harvest, both of which require planning and hard work. What's the difference? Tomatoes produce in a single season while a peach tree may not produce fruit for years, however, a peach orchard can produce fruit for years whereas a tomato plant must be replanted every season.

It may take longer than you've planned to see the harvest, to pick the fruit of your labor. Take heart, the fruit will taste that much better when you arrive.

Goals

"A goal without a plan is just a wish." - Anonymous

"Setting goals is the first step in turning the invisible into the visible." - Tony Robbins

Goals have been discussed in personal development circles for decades. I have my theory why most people don't have them, but none are legitimate. There are three common denominators during the most successful times in my life. I had a relationship with Jesus, a healthy body and written goals.

I was a dual-sport athlete in high school. To keep us on track the coaches would post weightlifting, conditioning, and speed goals on the metal double doors of the weight room. I looked at my power clean goal of 285 pounds every time I entered the weight room. It was much higher than my personal best of 240 pounds, but the coach set it there because he believed with the proper summer training, I could see a substantial increase.

Each day, even when I didn't feel like working out, I got dressed, walked into the weight room and stared at my goals. I worked hard all summer, and through perseverance and persistence, I reached this goal before the football season began.

Leadership is about setting the bar high and never giving up. It's about creating goals and pushing towards them. As a leader, I reflected on my high school success and knew goals had to be part of the plan. When I began searching for goal templates, most searches led me to "SMART goals," and this worked temporarily. But SMART goals don't encourage people to dream big.

The SMART acronym stands for "Specific, Measurable, Achievable, Realistic and Time-based." As I set goals, the attainable and realistic parts didn't sit well with me.

Had my coaches given me an attainable, realistic goal in high school, they would have said 260 versus 280 pounds. They set it higher because they wanted me to push past what I thought was possible. They set a bold goal because they believed in me and wanted to push my potential.

My decision to be physically, financially, emotionally, and spiritually healthy at 60 years old is not based on my past performance. Anyone who knew me then would laugh at the absurdity of the idea. This decision was based on what I believed I would accomplish if I set my mind to the goal and established a system to get there.

When I set the goal to become a professional speaker, I knew I would need to leave my job. This was a BIG, BOLD idea. It did not feel attainable and when I counted the cost, it didn't feel realistic either.

When I set the goal to write a book, despite my literary shortcomings, I was bombarded with the familiar feelings of inadequacy and uncertainty. It was the most unrealistic idea I'd had since quitting my job to be a professional speaker. Yet here I am, and here it is, my BIG goal in black and white.

Life isn't about doing what's attainable; it's about dreaming big and passionately pursuing it. If you fall short, at least you failed while trying. Your inner critic will always discourage your progress and those looking on from their safe, uninspiring perches will cast their share of doubt, but according to Theodore

YOUR INNER CRITIC WILL ALWAYS SEEK TO DISCOURAGE YOUR PROGRESS.

Roosevelt, the critic doesn't count.

During a passionate speech titled, "Citizenship in a Republic," Roosevelt delivered the notable passage referred to as The Man in the Arena.

> It is not the critic who counts; not the man who points out how the strong man stumbles, or where the doer of deeds could have done them better. The credit belongs to the man who is actually in the arena, whose face is marred by dust and sweat and blood; who strives valiantly; who errs, who comes short again and again, because there is no effort without error and shortcoming; but who does actually strive to do the deeds; who knows great enthusiasms, the great devotions; who spends himself in a worthy cause; who at the best knows in the end the triumph of high achievement, and who at the worst, if he fails, at least fails while daring greatly, so that his place shall never be with those cold and timid souls who neither know victory nor defeat.

You have what it takes. You are the man or woman in the arena who has dared to fail greatly, but you need a plan and systems to organize your dreams. Doing so will increase the likelihood of success.

SMAT Goals

I prefer SMAT goals over SMART goals. SMAT goals are specific, measurable, accountable, and time-bound.

The American Society of Training and Development (ASTD) found people are 65% more likely to reach their goals when they've shared them with someone else. Accountability boosts chances of achieving goals. ASTD also found people are 95% more likely to reach their goals when they share them with a group and meet regularly to review them.

In order to produce your organization's abundant harvest, it's going to require less "achievable and realistic" goals and more accountability for those big, hairy, audacious goals.

Let's look at how to design a SMAT goal and then you'll have a chance to strategize what this looks like for you. Dream BIG and go beyond what you think is possible for you to produce.

Leadership Pipeline

Michael must produce a leadership pipeline and place two new team members in leadership roles by August 16. He arrives at this goal after recognizing operational interruptions due to lack of potential leaders within the organization. There is typically only one site manager, and his goal is to develop two more leaders to prepare for the upcoming holiday rush.

When talking with Michael, we begin by visualizing this process and outcome.

- Sit for 15 minutes and begin seeing the new leaders in position. What does this feel like?
- How will this help the individuals and their families?
- How will the organization benefit?
- Visualize each person or group improving because this is taking place.
- Take a deep breath and exhale slowly.
- What emotions do you feel?
- See them performing at high levels in their new positions.
- Where will you host the celebration dinner?
- What will you eat and drink?
- Taste and savor this moment.

Visualize what it would look like to achieve the goal and revisit this image daily. The next step is to assess the costs. Here is an example.

Time - creating a Leader in Training (LIT) program will cost you time. It may require 1 hour per day for 30 to 45 days or 4 hours per day for two weeks. Another option is to hire a training consultant to design this program for you. Executing the program could require an additional two to three days per week until the LIT candidate completes the program.

Money - Developing people is expensive and time consuming, but the return on investment, or ROI, will surpass the initial cost. Michael must account for this up front cost and also adjust the salary commensurate with the new leadership position.

People - Everyone won't favor your LIT nominees. A team member may leave the organization because of your decision, which will result in another hire and additional personnel costs. Be prepared for the negative feedback that often comes when someone feels slighted or overlooked. Remember, you're creating good soil and a learning culture produces better results. Look for opportunities for healthy conflict resolution and open communication.

MICHAEL'S SMAT GOALS

Specific - Place two team members (internal or external) in leadership roles within six months.

Measurable - Can someone unfamiliar with the situation measure if two new team members were placed by August?

Accountability - Have a conversation with five potential candidates expecting at least two to be ready by August. Schedule monthly check-ins with direct reports to show progress with each LIT candidate. Create a friendly wager if this doesn't happen, like the winner gets free dinner, the loser has to volunteer 10 additional hours, or the loser has to shave their head.

Time bound - LIT program completed by August 16. When coaching organizations to create LIT programs, I encourage them to break down break the large goal into smaller steps, then create a plan for each step. For example, the LIT program would consist of an LIT outline, initial communications, LIT program design, LIT program implementation, ongoing communications, LIT evaluation, LIT program celebration announcement and ceremony and a post-program evaluation. Each part would consist of smaller goals which will form the end result.

By having a clear plan laced with accountability, producing an abundant harvest will become a reality. You may be thinking, "What do I do if I don't have an accountability partner?"

Pay for one. My greatest leadership investment was paying for coaches and programs who taught me and held me accountable to my goals. I've paid tens of thousands of dollars during the first years of my business, but the ROI is typically more than 10:1.

Friends and co-workers may agree to hold you accountable as well, for free. If this is the route you choose to take be sure to define what accountability looks like, what questions you'd like them to ask, and how often you'd like them to ask them.

When choosing where and with whom to share your goals with, you can't tell your million dollar ideas to a nickel minded person. They will not comprehend your big, hairy, audacious, goals and they may end up discouraging you from achieving your dreams. If you need a safe place to share but a challenging place to grow through accountability, feel free to join our Seeds to Success private Facebook Group by scanning the QR code. Here you'll connect with like-minded leaders looking to produce an abundant harvest in their professional and personal lives. It's a place where you'll experience inspiration and mentorship.

A wise leader knows when to stick with the plan and when to deviate. A plan is not an ultimatum. It is simply a guiding star shining ahead to show where to go.

Now go, find your north star.

HARVEST IMPLEMENTATION EXERCISE

What do you want to produce? Complete this statement:

_____ must produce _____.
       (Name)   (Harvest)

Set aside 15 minutes in an environment free of distractions. It doesn't have to be free of noise but it should be full of what you need to visualize your harvest being produced. As you visualize, identify and see the event taking place. Identify each emotion and write it out.

1. What do you hear?
2. What do you see?
3. What do you smell?
4. What impact will this have on you?

When you produce this item, how will this help others and you?

Hold this idea in your mind and say out loud, "I produced _____ and now I am able to be _____ for others."

Use the space below to complete your SMAT goals.

Specific - Does it include specific numbers, people, places, etc? (I want to take a vacation vs. I want my immediate family to take a two-week vacation to Puerto Rico)

Measurable - Can your result be measured?

Accountability - Who will you allow to hold you accountable? How often will you meet to discuss progress? What happens when benchmarks aren't met?

Time Bound - When is the deadline to produce this?

Download the free one-year goal sheet by scanning QR code.

CHAPTER 7
Preparing the Garden

Would it make sense for a farmer to scatter seeds in an unprepared garden? Of course not.

A farmer understands for a seed to take root and bloom to its full potential, they must prepare the soil by removing the impediments and adding amendments to promote growth. Just as absurd as it would be for a gardener to skip the prep work, the same is true with your own growth and that of the team you lead.

Benjamin Franklin is quoted as saying, "By failing to prepare you are preparing to fail." In our fast-paced society, we want to skip the preparation and experience immediate success. Any accomplished musician would tell you this isn't possible. The piano player doesn't start by playing Beethoven's "Fur Elise". They start by playing "Twinkle, Twinkle, Little Star", or they may even start by learning something called scales.

Everyone loves to learn how to play a song, nobody wants to practice their scales. Scales are the set of musical notes in order according to pitch and learning how to navigate these scales is fundamental to musicianship. Learning scales prepares you to play more challenging songs, adapt to key changes, and play with other musicians.

Prepping the garden isn't fun. Farmers would much rather just reap the harvest, but that's not how life works. Preparation isn't easy or glamorous. As a matter of fact, it's the most labor-intensive, non-rewarding part because there are no fruits to immediately enjoy. And because it requires the most back-breaking work and the most gut-wrenching dedication, many stop after the planning stage.

Prep work is hard, but if you embrace hard you will produce a healthier and more abundant harvest. Trust the process and don't give up!

Unfortunately, some of the most challenging ground to prepare is found within us. As a leader, it's our responsibility to lead others but self-leadership is top priority. To come face to face with your inadequacies and still move forward is a trait very few leaders possess. Inviting accountability and honest feedback can be uncomfortable and sometimes painful, but it is the only way to grow.

The most difficult part of my life was overcoming addiction and a self-defeating mindset to be the father, husband, brother, son, and leader I was capable of. As I mentioned earlier, I allowed the weeds of life — drugs, procrastination, feeling inadequate, and a lack of organization — to overtake my life's garden. Every minute, dollar, and skill was wasted because I didn't take time to do the prep work. I had resigned myself to the idea that my garden would never produce anything other than the weeds that were choking out my potential. When people who cared about me confronted my dysfunctional mindset and challenged me to become better I turned the corner. I was able to look past the current state of my garden and visualize a better way. A better end result.

What are Weeds?

Different people struggle with different weeds, but there are commonalities found within them all. Weeds are habits, people, or things that stop one from producing his or her full potential.

For me, it was an addiction. It nearly robbed me of my family, my career, and my life. What are your weeds? Once they are identified you can proceed to remove them and create a space for positive growth.

Weeds will rob you of your passion. It's not that we don't want to be successful. We do. We desire success, we desire greatness, we desire progress. It may start off wonderfully as we begin snatching good fortune from the grip of this evasive rogue called life. Our imaginations burst out of complacency as we dream of a future for ourselves that extends far beyond the prosaic to prodigiousness.

Out of the dream appears our fuel called passion and we often return to this emotional pump to refill when our imagination begins to wane. But when the dream begins to fade and our grip on life loosens and the passion we once embraced becomes drab and mundane, we need to examine our garden. Chances are, weeds have crept in unnoticed and started robbing our soil of its nutrients, crowding out the good stuff. Here is a brief list of examples to get you thinking about yours.

- Procrastination
- Negative self-talk
- Gossip
- Associating with negative people
- Lack of physical activity
- Making excuses
- Lack of vision
- Poor eating habits
- Assuming the worst about yourself and others

Whether your weeds are found in the list above or you've identified another, it's imperative to take the steps to pull the weeds. Pulling the weeds makes the environment cultivate a place for your harvest to thrive.

How to Pull Weeds

Habits, people, and things don't suddenly take over our lives. It's a gradual process. As the weeds grow unmonitored, they invade every part of our lives. The overtaking is so gradual it almost appears as if they belong there. It's not until we find ourselves on the verge of destruction do we look back and wonder what happened.

A weed doesn't die until it's pulled up from the root. If you only address what's on the surface you'll never find true freedom. The same destructive behavior will emerge time and time again, often more aggressive than before. Depending on the severity of your weed problem, you may need to consult a professional. Seek help because you can't do it alone.

When I began the process of producing a healthy 60-year-old Joe, who had the energy and the stamina to run after my grandchildren and finances to entertain them, I knew I had to remove excessive drinking and drug use, consistently exercise, and limit excess consumption of unhealthy foods.

Each vice made me feel good in the moment, but they were short-term pleasures that ultimately endangered my long-term plan's success. My intrinsic motivation replaced the bad habits and my vision to see a healthier husband, father, leader and one day a grandfather prevailed. The thoughts of not being able to run around and live my days filled with joy drive me to make better choices. When exercising seems like a chore and I'm tempted to skip my routine, I envision myself having a conversation with the version of me I want to be later in life. The better me is because I choose to sow more productive seeds than harmful seeds.

During my recovery, I learned the saying, "Win one day at a time." This means not to rest on yesterday's success or failure but simply win today. Don't worry about tomorrow, just win today. It is a great reminder to take small steps and win one day at a time.

There are times I don't win the day. I still fail, but I pick myself up and keep moving forward. Abraham Lincoln once said, "The best thing about the future is that it comes one day at a time."

Another political giant, Winston Churchill, said, "Success is not final; failure is not fatal. It is the courage to continue that counts."

I was able to personally improve by winning one day at a time, which enabled me to better lead my family and organization.

You can't lead others when you struggle to lead yourself. Every great leader practices a supreme amount of self-discipline. Former U.S. President Theodore Roosevelt said, "With self-discipline most anything is possible." Will you be self-disciplined to pull the weeds?

The same theory applies to work culture. Weeds grow rampant in many organizations. If the organization has existed for a long time and the work culture hasn't improved, leaders will grow accustomed to the weeds, even expectant of them. They turn a blind eye to the weeds and simply hope their organization moves up and to the right. When weeds become normal, toxic behaviors soon follow.

I helped Michael, the leader who wanted to create a leadership pipeline, identify the weeds before implementing a plan. We had to assess the current and past struggles he faced when presenting new ideas. He explained anytime a new program was introduced, frontline members made a sweep of negative attacks.

History showed the administration provided moral and financial support in the beginning of a new program launch, but as the program moved forward, support faded and the program lost momentum needed for completion.

By identifying the weed, we were able to pull it before taking action.

We identified negative criticism and wavering support as weeds. This was addressed and pulled before we planted the seed of a LIT program. The actions, habits, and perception had to be extracted from the environment so the project could succeed.

Manure Makes Fertilizer

Mushroom compost is said to be the best organic fertilizer for growing vegetables. There are multiple formulas but common ingredients include soil, hay, shredded tree bark, and cow manure. Manure? Yep, good ol' poop!

If nature's best fertilizer is meant to include aged manure, your best ingredient to produce unfathomable results will require your past caca to be processed in order to feed personal and professional growth.

The smells of past mistakes have a stench like cow manure, but when allowed to age and process properly, mistakes, like cow manure, can be the greatest amendment for your organization's soil to promote optimal growth.

Authentic leadership stems from owning one's mistakes and being true to who you are as a person at home and at work. This style of vulnerability is essential to leadership growth. Owning mistakes and admitting fault publicly are only a part of the process, allowing failures to be used as fertilizer as opposed to being used against you. Apologizing when needed, and demonstrating lessons learned can be a catalyst for change.

A leader's ability to own up to his past mistakes and grow from them showcases their humility, confidence, and self-awareness. The ability to publicly demonstrate how you're working through the failure strengthens others through transparency and vulnerability. You learn life's greatest lessons through failure.

YOU LEARN LIFE'S GREATEST LESSONS THROUGH FAILURE.

In his role as Mike McDermott in the movie Rounders, Matt Damon quoted Jack King in "Confessions of a Winning Poker Player," "Few players recall big pots they have won, strange as it seems, but every player can remember with remarkable accuracy the outstanding tough beats of his career."

Failures don't have to stand out with pain. The lesson learned becomes the winning play you make as a leader. Give yourself grace walking through it and see the lessons you and others can reap from it. Once you own it and allow the failure to age a little, the lessons learned will fertilize others and become the soil for your comeback story.

I had to pull the weeds in my garden, whether it was my addiction, procrastination, or poor self-talk. Whatever robbed me of my resources or potential had to be identified and uprooted.

The willingness to accept responsibility, find solutions and then share this process with others builds connection, and connection is where magic happens!

I have yet to share my leadership shortcomings and process to victory in a keynote and not have people approach me afterwards. They are thankful because they have a newfound hope for their own personal journey. It may even give them context to support family members or friends who are struggling with a similar circumstance. You don't have to give up on someone just because they've given up on themselves.

Manure is the greatest growth stimulator because it can empower others and set them free. For others to be set free, you, my friend, must own your mistakes, learn from them, and commit to overcoming them. You can't just go out and share your failure right away. It needs to age. You need time to process what led to those mistakes, what you have learned from them, and how you will structure your life to not repeat the mistake.

Most of us don't make three hundred mistakes. We make the same mistake three hundred times. When you are able to pull the weed up by its root you'll break the cycle. The good news is once the old cycle is broken a new one can begin. Every good counselor will insist that when you remove one bad habit, you have to insert a good habit, because where there is a void, something will always fill in that space. If you pull the weeds out of the ground, well, another weed will creep back in or something else will take root in that open space. It's natural.

As you begin pulling your weeds, make a list of habits you'd rather have. Maybe you'd like to become a voracious reader, write books, or become a jazz connoisseur. This is the beauty found in taking control of your own garden. You can grow whatever you want.

Manure needs to sit in a compost pile to break down all its harmful elements. If it's added to the plants right away, it will burn and kill the plants. But if it's processed properly over time, it breaks down and becomes the greatest fertilizer. The same thing holds true when you allow mistakes to age. When the time is right your failure will be someone's blessing.

Once you know you've learned from your failure and have broken its destructive cycle, you can share it with your team. How you overcame your mistakes will become a teachable lesson used to promote growth and prepare a caring, kind culture.

HARVEST IMPLEMENTATION EXERCISE
Preparation

Answer this question below. What's robbing you of producing the results you desire at work and in life?

Once you've identified the weed, follow steps 1-3:

1. Identify the root cause.

2. Begin removing the weed by its root. The length of time it's been there (root depth) will determine the amount of energy required to remove it from your daily life.

3. Once removed, replace the weed with a better habit. (See next chapter about planting the seeds.)

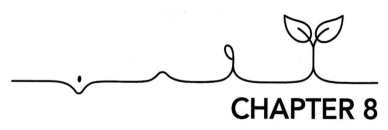

CHAPTER 8
Plant

A n unplanted seed never grows. I was never sure of myself. I had to battle doubts and fears daily. Could I really
overcome my personal struggles and be the leader I was
destined to be? Was it in me?

Time did not stand still amidst my struggles. Procrastination
only delayed the inevitable. Each waning dream led to another
day without action. Each day without action led to another unfulfilled dream. And each unfulfilled dream led to delayed potential.

After a year of winning against my inner demons, I decided
to make the move and take action. I had the vision and I had already created a plan to create a leadership development program
and establish leadership tiers to support operations.

The prep work had been completed as I pulled the weeds
that robbed me of the resources needed to produce healthy yields
at work. I had more work to do, but I cleaned ample space where
growth could take place and had given time for the past failures
to age and process into fertilizer for the upcoming plans.

I noticed that our organization had a gap and could benefit from a harvest of new leaders, but I also recognized the need to develop who we had in place. If we could pull this off, it would serve the organization's mission and people for years to come.

While I didn't have all the answers, I knew a seed needed to be planted, and that's exactly what I did. It started with identifying a process to successfully onboard new hires. We hosted live half-day training sessions on the second floor of the finance department building. I carried snacks, pens, computers and new hire folders a few hundred feet to the neighboring building and excitedly taught new team members what to expect and how they could contribute to the organization's success.

We continued the weekly training sessions, built, and adapted as the months went on. Onboarding transitioned into creating training manager positions to host new hires in their kitchens and to assist with other department training needs. A training manager program spilled over into the development of a new role — assistant managers. Each new initiative improved operations and, more importantly, developed new leadership opportunities.

It all started with one action and grew into something bigger. One tomato seed has the potential to produce enough food for a family of four for weeks. One tomato contains a couple hundred seeds that can yield hundreds of pounds of tomatoes over a few seasons, but the exponential growth only happens when the first seed is planted.

Hardware stores stock shelves with flower and vegetable seed varieties during growing seasons. A seed packet can contain anywhere from ten to a hundred seeds. It's safe to say, a seed packet has the potential to produce hundreds of pounds of produce. The seed packet can bring beauty to a yard or food to a kitchen table, but if it stays on the shelf, it will never reach its full potential.

We've established that in gardening and in leadership, there must be a farmer. The farmer is responsible for taking action. Leaders take action by planting the seed in order to achieve growth. Taking action is one of the most important steps to organizational growth because without implementation, growth potential can never be realized.

Action causes a sleepy seed to activate. Everything your organization needs is inside of your team members. It's up to the leader to cultivate growth within each person. When people are engaged, potential is released. When potential is freed, each person can produce results your organization desires and believes are possible.

When a farmer refuses to plant, the best ideas are left on the shelf and the growth of the organization is effectively abandoned. Identifying your limitations can speed up the process. While many things cause one not to take action, there are two common factors — doubt and paralysis by analysis.

"Doubt kills more dreams than failure ever will." - Suzy Kassem

Doubt is the greatest enemy to action. It causes us to stall and wait for "better conditions." In reality, there will never be a perfect time to act. Lack of confidence causes second guessing and doubt leads to unnecessary obstacles. The best advice is to do it scared. It sounds contradictory but in order to start you have to trust there is greater harm in not trying than actually taking action.

Doubt is a muscle built over time, but so is confidence. Directed action can strengthen your confidence. Don't delay. Act now and doubt will flee.

Paralysis occurs by analysis. Acting without planning can wreak havoc but overthinking and underdoing can be just as detrimental. If a farmer only thinks about what could go wrong in the future, he will never reap a harvest.

Our brains create worst case scenarios that are unlikely to ever occur. With each new scenario, another day of inaction goes by. One can only predict so many factors during the planning stage. The rest is revealed as action is taken.

Sometimes starting can be the hardest part. If you've ever driven a motorcycle you'll understand that the bike doesn't move as nimbly when it is standing nearly still, but once it starts moving the turns become practically effortless. Things that are in motion are simply easier to move. Just start. Don't overthink it. You have the plan, now execute.

Sometimes you have to do it scared until you are no longer scared to do it. Leading like a farmer demands you take action now. It is best to act and adapt than to never move at all. You've done the prep work. It's time to reap the harvest. It's time for the seeds you've planted to produce greatness.

Days to Germination

All vegetable seeds have various "days to germination". The number of days is often found on a seed packet. The amount of time for germination varies depending on the species. Days to germination is the amount of time a seed requires to become a seedling. Basically, it's when a seed moves from a dormant state to an awakened state, showing the first signs of its potential.

Just because you've taken the bold step to act does not mean the result will be immediate. It is wise to build a "germination" phase into your planning. This way you'll not get discouraged when your dreams don't emerge as quickly from the soil as you'd hoped. An unrealistic time-frame of implementation and execution can discourage your team and erode your believability. Trust is crucial when leading others so be sure to plan for germination and manage expectations.

Watering the Seed

The prep work has been done properly. The weeds have been pulled. The soil has been turned, and the compost has been added. Your seed has a better chance to reach its potential. Now the work really begins

What do you do after you've made the decision and planted the seed?

A seed needs several things to go from a sleepy seed to a fruit producing plant, able to support future generations. It is now up to the leader to decide the daily course of action. Remember, daily habits direct and engage people and promote healthy organizational growth.

Growing your organization and your personal development requires daily watering. In the early stages, a seed must stay damp at all times. This is similar to the life of a newborn baby. When a baby is first born, it needs to be fed frequently, constantly watched, and monitored more than in any other stage in a human's life.

A seed in the initial stages is most vulnerable and the risk of failure is the highest. A leader who takes consistent action to nurture and provide the seed potential with what it needs daily will help the seed sprout its first growth. The fruit won't come until much later.

A seed first grows in the dark where it is not seen. It happens underground. First, the roots dig deep into the soil before sending out the first signs of growth for the public to see. Similarly, a leader must be content to develop themselves in the dark, quiet moments. Our personal development transforms us into a more advanced, emotionally intelligent leader. It happens in the quiet times.

If a seed first establishes a strong root system, why would we think leadership, organizational growth, and personal development would be any different?

I did not change my life so that others would notice and praise my choices. I made the change for me and my family. I made the change because I was not realizing my potential. People will praise the public results but never know the private sacrifice.

I grew in the early morning hours when no one was watching. I grew late at night when no one was watching. I grew throughout the day when no one was watching.

I knew when I first invested in personal development that others would doubt the validity of my dream. I had spoken about doing better for years, but my words were empty because my actions never changed. I had the greatest intentions but they were paving the road to nowhere.

In the early years of my recovery, I found myself waking up at 3:45 a.m. every morning. It is very dark at those hours. No one is awake. Even the interstates are relatively empty. The gym parking lot had only a handful of cars and not many people inside, but I was planting positive seeds in order to develop my full potential. I knew for me to be a successful leader, I had to take care of my physical well-being.

While I took care of my physical body I also fed my soul. During those gym times when no one noticed me, I threw on my headphones and listened to motivational leaders like Eric Thomas, Inky Johnson, Les Brown, John Maxwell, Tony Robbins, and Ed Mylett. I'd shuffle from their teachings to sermons by Tony Evans and Myles Munroe. My seeds were actively growing in the dark, unseen, but full of potential.

When we plant the seed, we must water it daily. What daily disciplines do you need to implement? What does accountability look like for you? I focused primarily on my physical and spiritual growth in the beginning stages of my personal and professional development. I believe that doing less will enable you to focus with greater intensity. Don't try to change everything at once. Behavior modification, healthy habits, and productive thought patterns take time. If I tried to tackle financial, physical, emotional, mental, and spiritual goals all at once, I would become overwhelmed and want to quit.

Make some small changes and celebrate the wins. With each victory you'll build confidence to take on more, to transform more, to sow more seed. Instant results are not real. The harvest is a result of a persistent, disciplined life. The actions will not feel mundane when you can see how they form the bigger picture.

The habits you'll need to form will depend on your growth level and what it is you desire to produce. Regardless, your success will require daily action until you and your organization matures, similar to how a teenager needs less attention than a newborn. Both require attention but the amount and intensity changes.

INSTANT RESULTS ARE NOT REAL. THE HARVEST IS THE RESULT OF THE PERSISTENT, DISCIPLINED LIFE.

When people see you spray water on dirt they may laugh. All they see is mud, but what you're actually doing is creating a healthy environment for your seed to take root and run deep into the soil.

The healthier the roots, the healthier the fruits. People laugh because they see you watering dirt, but they don't understand you planted a seed. You are not watering dirt, you are watering your future.

Some thought my early morning routine was unnecessary. We both lacked understanding. They couldn't understand why I would get up so early and I couldn't understand why they didn't.

People may mock you in the planting stage because they haven't seen the fruit. In a results-driven world, we confuse results with success. True growth happens in the process. The fruits are a byproduct of commitment to the process.

It isn't until they see the fruit of your work that they believe in you as a leader.

Insects and Diseases

Farmer Katie taught a valuable lesson one fall day as we tended a garden row. The conversation started about how important morning routines are and how this is our time for deep, focused work. She shared her weekly farm chores.

She explained how she cleans and maintains the goat area on Mondays. Wednesdays are for inspecting the farm for insects and diseases. Fridays are for mowing the grass and weeding the garden spaces.

A puzzled look came over my face and my brain waves were firing in overdrive. "Whoa, whoa, whoa, what did you say you do on Wednesdays?" I asked.

"I go around the farm and check for insects and diseases," she said.

"Katie, I think I know the answer why on a farm you would want to check for insects and diseases, but could you just explain it to me?"

Katie's farm has a single lane, gravel driveway that runs nearly 500 yards from the gate entrance to her house. She drives past the planted areas and the outdoor classroom regularly, but her agricultural mind sees more than a budding plant.

"I drive on this road every day and I can see that the sunflowers are growing. I can see the little tomatoes starting to pop off the vines, and they're starting to turn red. I can see some of the squash blossoms are starting to open. So, from the road, it looks like everything's doing what it should be doing. And from the road I would be right. But every Wednesday I look for insects and diseases because, even though I can see positive results from afar, it doesn't mean that something isn't right up on top of a crop, tearing it away."

How often do you simply measure success by seeing the fruits?

This is extremely dangerous to the organization. Ongoing care is needed to protect the fruits so they can be harvested. Insects and disease can slowly destroy all organizational success.

- Do you have a daily habit of checking for critters who are looking to rob you of your harvest?
- Is there something you need to get close and personal to see?
- Do you need to do a deep dive into financials or metrics to evaluate the health of your organization?
- What questions are you asking your direct reports to get a healthy overview of your organization?

On the surface things may look fine, but what you don't see are the little insects and diseases that are inside of your organization eating away at the hard work, time and money invested to produce a healthy harvest.

You must be intentional about checking for organizational insects and diseases. I don't always see the little Japanese beetles eating my green beans in the garden. I only see them when I get up close and examine the plants each week.

The truth is, your opponents want your crop. Do you want it more? Are you willing to let someone, or something, steal it away? As a practice, for the next six months I'd like you to:

- Schedule a day every week on your calendar. Label it "inspect for insects and diseases."
- Look closely at your team and examine behaviors, tension, or gaps.
- Pay attention specifically to what's promoting or stifling growth.

- Look at yourself. What is trying to rob you of your potential and your results?

As you inspect, you may not see anything the first week. It may not be there next week. It may not be there three weeks later, but the moment you ignore them, the insects will creep in. And once they find a home, they will take over the entire crop you worked so hard to produce.

Continuous Weeding Required

A farmer knows that once the seed has been planted, it needs to be watered. They also understand that you are constantly pulling weeds. We mentioned the back breaking work that needs to be done to prepare the soil for planting. However, just because the weed is pulled once doesn't mean that it's gone forever. Weeds love the same things seeds love — the sun, the water and the soil. They battle for the same resources.

As a leader, just because you created the new leadership development plan or started the training process doesn't mean that those old behaviors won't try to creep back into the space.

Special attention must be given to the weeds that want to creep back into your space intended for growth. Be aware and stay vigilant because it's there. Both seeds and weeds sprout from healthy soil and initially you may not be able to discern the difference. The seed and the weed can look the same in the early stages. The best leader knows how to identify the seed they planted from the familiar foe that attacks and robs all their resources.

As the seed sprouts, you must be very mindful to water it and pull back the weeds. Don't give up because you are days away from a breakthrough. Don't be the person who walks away right before that little seed is about to sprout through the dirt.

Leaders, be mindful of these situations. Be mindful that your diligence is needed, your persistence is needed, but more than anything, your faith and patience is needed because you are about to see the growth. It's so close.

Then as the seedling continues to mature, you want to be mindful of next steps. There are additional actions to take from the time you see the seed break through earth's crust to the time it produces fruit.

A tomato plant is a very funny vine. It appears as if there are little hairs coming off the stem but they are actually roots. As the plant reaches towards the sun, offshoots spring from the main stem. That little branch will hold the tomato.

Between the main stem and the branch another little thing grows. It's green and appears healthy. It looks like it should be there, but that little area is called a sucker. A tomato farmer knows that plucking the little sucker away from the main stem and the branch has benefits. If allowed, the sucker can suck away the nutrients intended for the fruit, leaving the branch depleted from what it needs to produce larger fruit. The plant is capable of producing with suckers present but fruits will be smaller. Pulling suckers make the plant more robust and manageable.

Become very mindful of the suckers inside of your organization that look like they're walking through the process, appearing to do what they need to do. They may be the people, processes, or systems depleting and diverting resources from the fruit.

Don't throw the sucker away. The sucker isn't the bad thing. It's just growing in the wrong space. A leader is responsible for removing the sucker and trying to replant it in a new area for healthy growth.

An actual tomato sucker can be plucked from the original plant, placed into a new environment, and can become a fruit producing plant.

Sometimes people need to be pulled out of a specific area that they may be in. Maybe they need to move departments. Maybe they need to move roles. It's not that they are bad, they're just in the wrong area, just like the tomato sucker. But once it is plucked from that area, then that project can produce the fruit that it's looking for. Take the sucker, put it into some new environment and let it take root there.

In his evergreen book Good to Great, Jim Collins uses a bus illustration which proposes three important questions.

1. Are the right people on the bus?
2. Are the wrong people off the bus?
3. Are the right people in the right seats?

Jim Collins explains,

> When Colman Mockler became chief executive of Gillette in 1975, he spent 55 percent of his time moving people around in seats on the bus. He got some people off, but most of it was trying to find the right seat for people. What he said is that just as a company has its three circles—he didn't use these terms, but it's essentially what he said—just as a company has its three circles, its passion, and its wiring (what it can be really outstanding at and maybe where it can best contribute, which translates into economics), individuals have their own three circles. Right? Where your passion lies, what you're genetically encoded for, and what you can contribute that is of value to the institution, which would be the analogy to the economic engine.
>
> The key as a manager is to find or construct seats where an individual's three circles line up with the needs and responsibilities of that seat. If you have the right person on the bus, but

they're in the wrong seat, they will fail or they'll certainly struggle. A lot of the task is to answer a very difficult question. If I've got a people problem here—even somebody who seemed right before, but now they're struggling—the first assumption, if you're trying to reach Level 5, is to assume that you as a manager have blown it. I'm the one who's responsible for their failing. I must have somehow—first line of defense—I must have failed by not preparing them for the seat, by not picking the right seat for them, by not recognizing the fact that the seat is much larger than what their capabilities are at the moment, whatever. Just sort of always assume you screwed up.

Second, though, is if you go through all that, and you still come to the conclusion that somebody is just the wrong person on the bus, you have to confront that fact. But if it's somebody who's really proven themselves in one seat and they're failing in another seat, there's somehow something that is wrong about either the seat selection or in the development process of that person for the seat.

Now, there is one caveat to all this, which is that if you watch organizations develop, sometimes what happens is a very uncomfortable situation. It's a brutal-facts situation. Whereas the bus gets larger and goes faster, the seats get bigger and more difficult. And at some point, somebody who had the capabilities to hold a particular seat on the bus—it outgrows them. They cannot fulfill the responsibilities of that seat for whatever sets of reasons. Something's changed in their life; they don't grow into it, whatever. There then comes a really difficult decision, which is usually taken in concert with them. Do you want to have a smaller seat, or do you really not want to be on the bus?

That's the nature of entrepreneurial growth. It happens in every entrepreneurial company that there are some people who were perfect when the bus was a little tiny minivan; and when it finally becomes a big Greyhound bus going down the road, they just—the seat is just too big for them. Part of the challenge as a manager is to really be right in answering the following question: can they grow into that seat or not?[1]

Jim Rohn said, "There are two types of pain we will experience in life, the pain of discipline and the pain of regret. The difference is that discipline weighs ounces while regret weighs tons."

In order to produce the results that you're looking for inside of your organization, in order to be the leader that you are destined and designed to be, you must be committed to the daily disciplines. Yes, it's hard. Yes, it's painful. But at the end of the day, it is way less painful than looking back years from now with regret because you didn't take the time to lead a disciplined life.

Discipline

Discipline has a negative connotation. But discipline creates freedom and it's the freedom we're all looking for. Discipline creates the freedom of choice, but it's only attainable if you're willing to commit yourself to the process.

Its disciplined gardener waters the plants, tends to the weeds, pays attention to the insects, and prunes the suckers every single day. Laziness allows for weeds, disease, and failed potential. You don't have time to be undisciplined. You are supposed to raise people up, not crush their potential. You are who you think you are, for better or worse. Why not think better and step into the person you were created to be?

It's your time to take over. Let them know that the harvest is coming.

HARVEST IMPLEMENTATION EXERCISE
Plant

What steps did you take to move closer to producing better results? *(planting seeds)*

What daily habits did you incorporate into your schedule? *(watering seeds)*

How did you keep the weeds from growing again? *(Continually pulling weeds)*

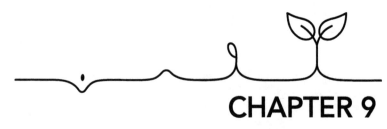

CHAPTER 9
Produce

T he goal is to produce fruit, right? Not exactly. The work has only just begun once the fruit appears. I mentioned earlier that my grandfather always planted a garden. Their house was perched atop a hill more than 20 feet above the highway, adjacent to their property. It was perfect for sun and drainage.

I remember looking out my grandparents' kitchen window and seeing huge barren clay ground. My grandfather would get on this tractor and plow it. Sometimes he would allow me to sit on the tire beside him, but often it was a little bit bumpy and too dangerous for me to sit there. So, I would stand inside of the kitchen and watch him.

THE WORK HAS ONLY JUST BEGUN ONCE THE FRUIT APPEARS.

He worked so hard to produce tomatoes, squash, green beans, okra, and cucumbers. I can still see the garden full of life. My grandparents grew up during the Great Depression and for his family, growing food was not a hobby but a necessity. I remember late July to early August the South Carolina temperatures would peak and the veggies would start to produce. The squash was already popping. My grandmother and I would go out into the field. I enjoyed that time with her.

My grandfather's hard work over the season started to pay off. He planned for this moment. He dedicated himself and worked the ground until his hands were calloused. He did everything required to prepare the soil for planting. He took action and placed each seed carefully in the soil and tended to it every day. He watered the garden, pulled the weeds, and inspected for any insects and diseases. And while many would think the work was over, it had really just begun.

My grandfather always did four things when it came time to harvest. He enjoyed some, saved some, gave some, and kept the seeds.

Enjoy Some

My grandfather made sure my grandmother sliced some of those tomatoes as soon as she picked them from the vine. We ate them that day for lunch or dinner. He wanted to be sure we enjoyed some of the initial fruit of our labor. He grew the garden to provide for his family. He did it so we would have food on the table.

I wasn't really keen on tomatoes back then, but now as an adult, a garden grown sliced tomato, still warm from the summer heat, sliced with a little salt and pepper on the side with my lunch is an all time favorite. I've learned how to truly enjoy the fruit.

Purpose driven leaders are forward thinking, rightfully so. They look to the next season and plan accordingly. One of the disadvantages of being too forward thinking is that you are unable to celebrate in the present.

Best-selling author Brendon Burchard notes, "It's the small wins on the long journey that we need in order to keep our confidence, joy and motivation alive."

Celebration is one of the key ingredients your organization needs to thrive. Refusing to give praise and celebrate small victories would be the equivalent to withholding water from the seed. You may not notice the negative impact in an hour, but you certainly will after a couple of days.

Enjoying the fruit of the labor accomplishes two goals. First, it slows us down. It forces us to pause from our labor, finding rest in our success. It's positive reinforcement to your team who may have just worked consecutive 60-70 hour weeks to finish an important project. When you tell them that the busyness is only a season, you'd better be prepared to back that up and reward their efforts. Maybe you give your hard working team a day off, take them on a day trip to a spa, attend a sporting event together, or take them out to a very nice dinner. The pause builds unity and communicates empathy within your organization.

The second thing that happens when you enjoy the fruits of your labor is gratitude. Your team will naturally feel proud of their accomplishment. But if you do not feel equally proud of their accomplishment and sacrifice, their joy will quickly turn sour. They'll no longer feel proud, they'll feel hopeless. The next time you ask them to go above and beyond you may not receive the same eager response.

Developing a culture of gratitude begins with the leader. American philosopher William James once said, "The deepest craving of human nature is the need to be appreciated." If this is true, then no bonus will ever truly satisfy. Take time to enjoy small victories. Your work culture will be better because of it.

So often we lose sight of enjoying the fruits of our work within our organizations. We reach a milestone or a goal and then we never celebrate it. There are plenty of studies showing that companies who celebrate their achievements will repeat them more frequently with even greater results. Praise what you want repeated.

If it was a leadership development pipeline, celebrate it. Celebrate the fact that you actually achieved this huge milestone. Make it a big deal because you now have what it takes in order to create sustainability inside of your organization.

Enjoy the fruits of your work. If you don't enjoy the fruits of the work, you become more and more depleted and you forget what it feels like to achieve the results that you desire.

Save Some

My grandparents would always save some of the harvest. They knew the garden would be unable to produce during the cold season.

I can still see my grandmother over the steaming pot, getting her Mason jars ready. She had a little rubber handle glass jar holder that she used to place the jars filled with the stewed tomatoes down into the boiling water.

Whenever you find yourself in a fruitful season, don't consume all you grow. Try to save some for the tough times. Billionaire Warren Buffett says it this way, "Do not save what is left after spending. Spend what is left after saving." We tend to get this backwards, don't we? Build in margin for yourself and your organization.

If you have never been good managing money or have received little to no financial education, I'd recommend starting with something achievable, like Dave Ramsey's Financial Peace. It will give you the framework needed to become financially stable and you may end up implementing some of the principles into your work life as well.

Give Some

My grandparents also faithfully gave some. My grandmother had two brothers and a sister who lived down the road and they had a bountiful harvest as well. They would always exchange some of their varieties. They enjoyed giving. They had visitors who would come from the church or community and they gave what they had in abundance.

I'm convinced that you'll never feel more alive than when you are giving back. Yes, it is a biblical principle found in Acts 20:35, but that's not all. According to Dr. Allen McConnell,

> Research by social psychologist Liz Dunn and her colleagues appearing in the journal Science shows that people's sense of happiness is greater when they spend relatively more on others than on themselves.
>
> In one survey of over 600 U.S. citizens, Dunn and colleagues found that spending money on others predicted greater happiness whereas spending money on oneself did not, and this pattern was found across all income levels. In other words, even those with little money reported greater happiness when their proportion of spending on others, relative to the self, was greater.[1]

Involving your team in charitable giving adds additional layers of purpose and satisfaction to their lives.

Keep the Seeds

My grandfather tied a white strip of cloth around one corn plant, one of the tomato plants and one of the okra plants, for example.

My grandmother always told me not to mess with those plants. Each of these specific plants had a purpose.

Every time I saw a white cloth, I thought about the universal sign for surrender — the white flag. I was tempted, but I listened.

I later realized my grandfather was saving that plant for seeds. In his day, you didn't go to the store and buy a pack of seeds. There are hundreds of seeds inside a tomato plant. Once they are dried they are perfect for planting.

He would dry it over the winter so that he could replant them the next year. If you enjoyed it all, there would be no seeds for next year's planting. If you gave it all away, there would be no seeds left for next year's planting.

You have to keep some seed so you can multiply the growth. There will be moments when your desired results are not being realized. To produce results day in and day out is unfathomable. It is impossible. It's an unrealistic expectation.

I've had people ask me, "Joe, what happens if I give it away and then somebody steals the idea and they go and do it."

I tell them, "Let someone take it and run with it." Most people don't have the discipline or the follow-through to take your idea and do something with it. That's a scarcity mindset. Don't believe the lie that you lose when you give something away. Giving things away is the quickest way to multiply your harvest.

No, you don't have to give away the entire recipe. Grandmothers don't give you the full recipe to their world-class apple pie. There is always a *secret ingredient* held back. They may say that secret ingredient is *love,* but you later find out it was cinnamon. Give enough to help people get going, and give beyond what you think is possible or needed.

You want to get your organization in a place where you are giving away the great things that you're doing. Put it in a PDF file. When you give value and content away, your organization becomes a flowing river of ideas and production.

145

The more you give away, the more people will give back to you. It becomes a cyclical process that benefits your members, your organization and your leadership, but then it starts to spill over into other areas across the world. So, yes, give some away.

Keep some of the seed so that you can influence leadership multiplication. You created a leadership development program so that you have a pipeline of leaders, excellent! There is seed in that fruit, potential to develop. Eventually, it will be their job to multiply the seed so that you can have an even greater, multi-layered leadership pipeline.

Whether you're talking about leadership development, a new training program, customer service, or a new marketing campaign, if you live by those four principles you will produce the results.

The final piece is the labor force. You must accurately discern how much later will be needed to harvest the produce. No farmer wants to leave fruit to die on the vine. It's symbolic of neglect, poor resource management, or laziness. None of those traits are enviable. It would be crushing to an organization to have toiled, developed, and seen the fruits of their labor but not be able to actually harvest the crop. The only way the fruit makes it to the market is if the laborers are ready to receive it.

We are once again back to the produce section in the grocery store. It's time to take all of the results that you've achieved to the right market so that you can go and set up your own produce section to enjoy the return on your investment.

HARVEST IMPLEMENTATION EXERCISE
Produce

Once your seeds to success produce, fill in the ways you'll do each of the following:

Enjoy Some:
How will you celebrate your accomplishment? Take time to cherish the moment, the victory, and appreciate the hard work it took to accomplish it.

Save Some:
Which portion of the success story will you hold onto and use for slower seasons?

Give Some:
To whom will you give your success to? How will you share your accomplishments with others?

Keep the Seeds:
Take the small idea and actions *(seeds)* that produced the results and repeat this step every year moving forward. Don't allow your success to be done in vain, but keep planting the same good habits that helped to achieve the first harvest.

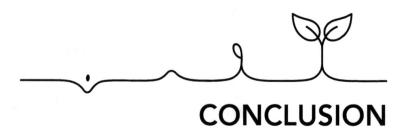

CONCLUSION

E very day the farmer makes the choice to get up and tend to their field, their crop, their produce. It's not easy to get up and toil day after day without immediate gratification unless you have faith. You have faith that if you did the right things, if you prepared the garden, cultivated the soil, created a safe environment for growth, and planted in the proper season, you will see a positive result.

Every day you will face the choice to quit or to press on. What will you choose? Some days are more daunting, more depressing than others. Some people face relational choices. Do you struggle through a difficult marriage, choosing to remain faithful, even if the current outlook is bleak? Can you have faith to believe your choice to continue cultivating the ground will one day result in a stronger, life-giving relationship?

Maybe you must make a professional choice. Will you stick with the safe, familiar job that has provided for your family and your future or will you risk everything to start your own business and pursue something you are truly passionate about?

Other choices stunt our spiritual growth. How we use our bodies, how we tame our tongues, and how we hold captive our thoughts are all choices that bear the weight of potential strife and division if left unchecked. In a picture-perfect world, we would prefer to not make these choices. We would choose for someone else to make the hard choice for us and that the outcome would always be favorable.

The analogy of two roads is clear. We are at the fork and can see for miles in every direction although we aren't certain of the destination at the end of either path. One road seems inevitably tougher than the other. The tougher road isn't enticing, it's frightening. It isn't attractive, it's repelling. It isn't accepting, it's confrontational. It's everything our born nature revolts against, but it's the very thing our blessed soul acknowledges as right.

We want to avoid difficulty and still build character and resolve, but this is not how growth works. Trials make us stronger, and courage arises as we conquer our fears.

As you read this book you may have either identified with the farmer or the seed. If you are leading others, you have to take responsibility for your garden. If there is something you don't like, change it. You are responsible for preparing the ground for exponential growth.

Some of you may have read this and felt more like the seed than the farmer. You know there is something great within you, but you don't know how to get it out. The initial growth of a seed is rather violent. The embryo must crack through its seed coat before the seedling can emerge and become what it was created to be.

Likewise, your life may require an abrupt, chaotic shift. Perhaps you have been hiding in the comfort of the proverbial seed coat but now it's time to break free. It's time to put the Seeds of Success Framework into action and stop blaming the market for not buying rotten fruit from your garden.

It took time to get rid of my weeds, those of alcoholism and drug addiction. If I can turn my life around, so can you. There is an orchard waiting inside of you, even if it feels like all you have is an insignificant seed.

As you embrace the nuances of this book, I want you to apply them, teach them and enjoy the fruits of your work.

Producing results is not a one-time thing, it's a learned process. Once you receive the results from the Seeds to Success Framework it becomes how you approach every aspect of your life and organization. Don't delay. Don't be like a seed inside of its packet sitting on the shelf. Make the choice to plan, prepare, plant, and produce your potential. The time to act is now.

It's. Not. Over.

ENDNOTES

Introduction
1. https://www.johnmaxwell.com/blog/the-law-of-the-lid/

Chapter 1:
1. Sinek, Simon. The Infinite Game. Penguin: 2019, 158.
2. https://www.bmc.org/nutrition-and-weight-management/weight-management
3. https://www.forbes.com/sites/forbesfinancecouncil/2021/09/13/why-investors-chase-gamestop-bitcoin-and-other-get-rich-quick-opportunities/?sh=5cb04f4f188f
4. https://www.lsuagcenter.com/profiles/lbenedict/articles/page1607970261368

Chapter 2:
1. Proverbs 27:17, NIV.
2. Brown, Brené. Daring Greatly: How the Courage to be Vulnerable Transforms the Way We Live, Love, Parent and Lead. London, England: Portfolio Penguin, 2013.
3. Willink, Jocko. Extreme Ownership: How U.S. Navy SEALs Lead and Win. New York: St. Martins Press, 2015.
4. Sinek, Simon. Leaders Eat Last: Why some teams pull together and others don't. New York: Portfolio/Penguin, 2014.
5. https://www.kent.edu/yourtrainingpartner/just-do-it-how-identify-and-address-8-levels-accountability

Chapter 3:
1. https://135704.fs1.hubspotusercontent-na1.net/hubfs/135704/2022%20Strengths%20Based%20Infographics/NFIFatherAbsenceInfoGraphic.pdf
2. Sinek, Simon. The Infinite Game. Penguin, 2019.

3. https://hbr.org/2018/01/how-you-promote-people-can-make-or-break-company-culture

4. https://www.gallup.com/workplace/247391/fixable-problem-costs-businesses-trillion.aspx

5. https://hbr.org/2015/12/proof-that-positive-work-cultures-are-more-productive

6. https://www.cnbc.com/2019/07/11/workers-value-a-strong-company-culture-over-higher-pay-study-claims.html

7. https://www.forbes.com/sites/nazbeheshti/2019/01/23/improve-workplace-culture-with-a-strong-mentoring-program/?sh=73d04eba76b5

8. https://warwick.ac.uk/newsandevents/pressreleases/new_study_shows/

9. https://impact.economist.com/perspectives/sites/default/files/EIU_Lucidchart-Communication%20barriers%20in%20the%20modern%20workplace.pdf

10. Gladwell, Malcolm. Tipping Point: How Little Things Can Make a.Big Difference. Boston: Back Bay Books, 2002.

11. https://www.bondcap.com/report/it15/#view/110

Chapter 4:

1. https://www.cnbc.com/select/73-percent-of-americans-rank-finances-as-the-number-one-stress-in-life/

2. USDA.gov – need actual website

3. https://www.ncl.ac.uk/business/news-events/news-items/embrace-sustainable-leadership/

Chapter 5:

1. https://en.wikipedia.org/wiki/Kairos#cite_note-3

2. https://www.statista.com/statistics/186833/average-television-use-per-person-in-the-us-since-2002/

3. https://en.wikipedia.org/wiki/Pomodoro_Technique

4. https://todoist.com/productivity-methods/pomodoro-technique

Chapter 6:

1. Jim Collins & Jerry Porras. "Built to Last: Successful Habits of Visionary Companies." Random House, 2005.
2. https://www.johnmaxwell.com/blog/a-new-definition-of-success
3. Clear, James. Atomic Habits: Tiny Changes, Remarkable Results: An Easy & Proven Way to Build Good Habits & Break Bad Ones. New York, New York: Avery, an imprint of Penguin Random House, 2018.

Chapter 8:

1. https://www.jimcollins.com/media_topics/inTheRightSeats.html

Chapter 9:

1. https://www.psychologytoday.com/us/blog/the-social-self/201012/giving-really-is-better-receiving

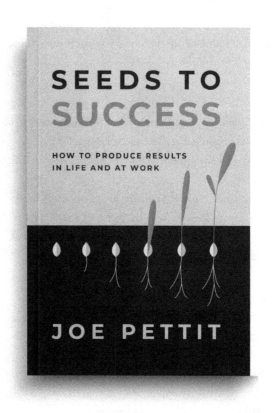

Free Resources Available at
www.joepettitinspires.com/book